# Dad's War

# Also by Marina Reznor

Kingsbury Town Football Club Romance Series
*Fowled (Book 1)*
*Booked (Book 2)*

# DAD'S WAR

MARINA REZNOR

An Army photographer, Lady Chatterley,
and the story of how whole blood helped win World War II

VOLUME I

KINGSBURY TOWN PRESS
BIRMINGHAM ALABAMA

All maps courtesy of the author.

Dad's War: an Army photographer Lady Chatterley, and the story of how whole blood helped win World War II - Volume I

Copyright © 2020 Kingsbury Town Press, all rights reserved.
First Kingsbury Town Press printing, October 2020

www.kingsburytownpress.com

Except where noted, all images the property of The Estate of Howard J Francis Jr.

Cataloging-in-Publication data record for this book is available from the Library of Congress.
ISBN:      978-0-9994297-8-5 (paperback)
           978-0-9994297-7-8 (eBook)

Library of Congress Control Number (LCCN): 2020941862

All rights reserved. No part of this book may be reproduced, transmitted, or utilized in any form or by any electronic, mechanical, or other means, now known or hereafter invented, including photocopying and recording, or in any informational storage or retrieval system, without prior permission in writing of the publisher.

Permissions: Every effort has been made to acknowledge correctly and contact the source and/or copyright holder of each item. The publisher apologizes for any unintentional errors or omissions, which will be corrected in future editions of this book.

Notice: Product or corporate names may be trademarks or registered trademarks and are used only for identification and explanation without intent to infringe.

Marina Reznor has asserted her right under the Copyright, Designs and Patents Act, 1988, to be identified as the author of this work.

*Cover design: Nick Venables Design*

*Editors: David Ballheimer, Angela Bell*

*Development editor: Howard Newstadt*

# Contents

| | | |
|---|---|---|
| Maps | | xi |
| Foreword | | xv |
| Preface | | xix |
| 1 | Dad had flat feet | 23 |
| 2 | Ma needs yeast | 29 |
| 3 | Keep your mouth shut, Georgie | 33 |
| 4 | Lady Chatterley | 39 |
| 5 | The crossing, in which Dad gets his own salmon for dinner | 43 |
| 6 | What you need to know about blood and war | 53 |
| 7 | The 2nd MAMAS set up shop | 59 |
| 8 | Major Hardin's problems | 81 |
| 9 | The meeting at Salisbury | 85 |
| 10 | Who the hell let TIME magazine in the door? | 91 |
| 11 | Blood begins to flow | 101 |
| 12 | "Everyone speaks French here. Even the little kids." | 113 |
| 13 | Across the Rhine | 133 |
| 14 | He's carrying the suitcase | 149 |
| | Epilogue | 163 |
| Acknowledgments | | 169 |
| About the author | | 171 |
| Bibliography and Further Reading | | 173 |

A FARMER ON A HILL SAID OF THE GERMANS, DO NOT SAY THAT IT HAD TO DO WITH THEIR LEADERS, THEY ARE A PEOPLE WHOSE FATE IT IS TO ALWAYS CHOOSE A MAN WHOM THEY FORCE TO LEAD THEM IN A DIRECTION IN WHICH THEY DO NOT WANT TO GO.

— GERTRUDE STEIN, WARS THAT I HAVE SEEN, 1945
DAD BECAME FRIENDS WITH GERTRUDE AT THE
US ARMY 203RD GENERAL HOSPITAL, GARCHES, FRANCE

# MAPS

North America, circa 1945 (Map 1)

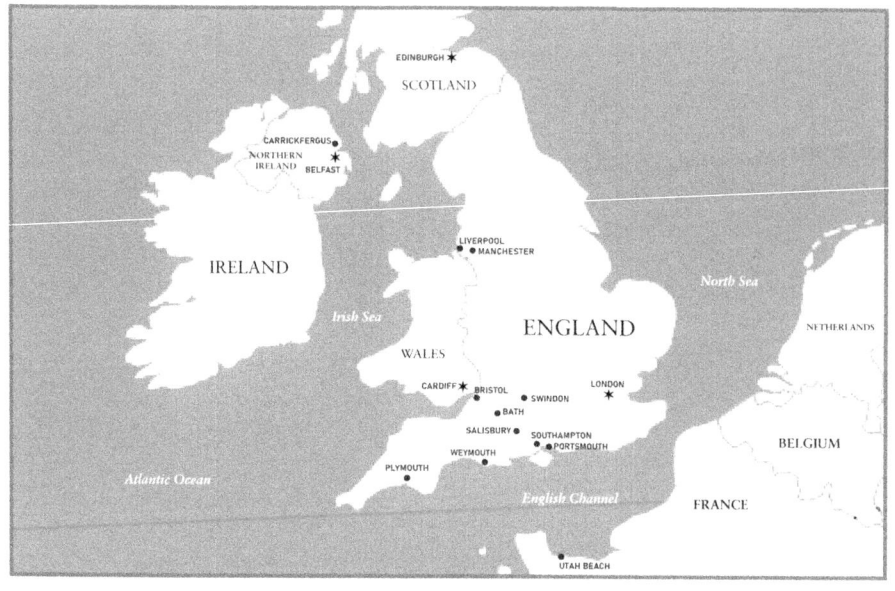

United Kingdom, circa 1945 (Map 2)

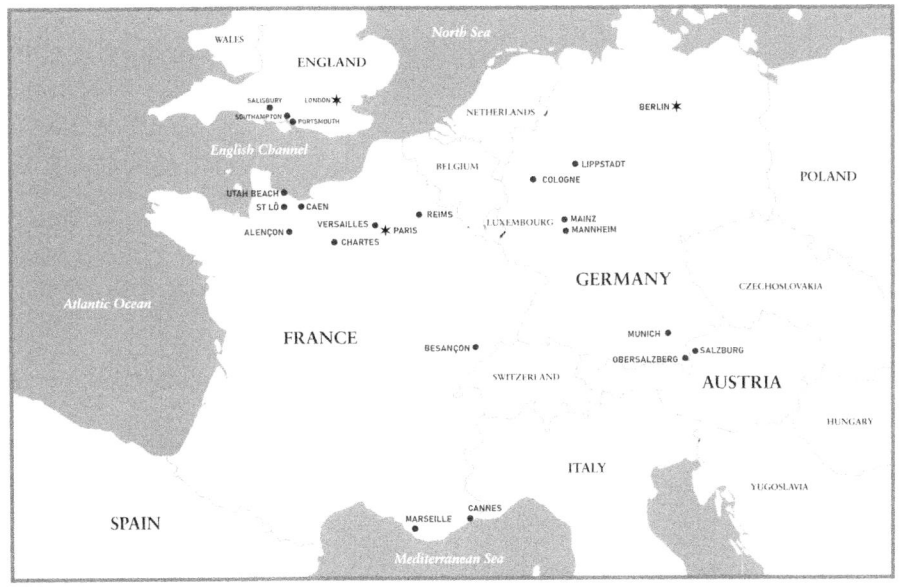

Europe, circa 1945 (Map 3)

# Foreword

As a retired Army officer, Vietnam veteran, and voracious reader who specializes in American military history, I have spent countless hours absorbing stories of the heroes of our country. Washington, Scott, Lincoln, Grant, Lee, Sheridan, Pershing, Eisenhower, Roosevelt, Bradley, MacArthur, Ridgeway, and Westmoreland among others who guided the mostly strategic decisions that led to the final outcome.

At a different level are the histories of actions of a tactical nature where soldier met soldier on the battlefield. From Roger's Rangers and Arnold's impossible trek through the Maine woods to capture Quebec, to Morgan's victory at Cowpens, Washington's at Yorktown, Sheridan's March to the Sea, and the campaigns of Patton in the final European campaigns, these are stirring tales.

World War II was an epic event in the world's history. As we mark the 75th Anniversary of the war's end in Europe, it is useful to reflect on the great men at the top of the various entities, both political and military, whose strategic decisions and guidance influenced the final outcome. Other histories, which tell a part of the story at Division, Regiment, or even Battalion level during the final year of the war in Western Europe, are also important in the individual character and performance they reveal. It is natural that most close-up accounts of these events deal with combat units and the challenges of being a participant.

The historic account contained in this book is somewhat different. A story contained deep in the huge essential support services that made the combat forces viable. This is the story of whole blood, its importance at forward hospitals for early treatment, and the development of methods to transport and store it effectively. The result was the saving of thou sands of wounded soldiers' lives.

But it is also the story of an average soldier whose great luck and talent in early training and assignments led to his participation in these significant events. Because he was the photographer of this unit, and had his own dedicated transportation, Howard J Francis Jr was in a special position to see and photograph much of the last year of the war in France and Germany from a non-combat role. Thus the highlight of this account is the large collection of unpublished photographs of that period.

I had the privilege of meeting Howard a few times in his later years. Our mutual interest in books and military history was a pleasant focus for conversation. I saw some of his photographs then, and have seen some more since, but to have them organized in this telling of his World War II story is the only way to fully understand and appreciate them and is a genuine delight. Every man and woman who contributed to the American war effort in World War II was a hero, and this is a story about one of them.

Colonel Richard E Helmuth, Retired<br>
Brunswick, Maine<br>
May 2020

Howard J Francis, Jr at Stonehenge, Wiltshire England, 1943 (Image Preface.1)

# Preface

My father, Howard J Francis Jr, would have been 100 years old this May. He got to see a lot of life, and said himself he was among those either blessed or cursed to live in interesting times.

This book is a collection of his photographs from World War II in the European theater of war. Dad was a US Army Technical Sergeant Fifth Class who served with the 2nd Museum and Medical Arts Service, which gave him a camera and an access pass to a part of the war rarely seen.

While his job as a medical photographer was important, Dad made no secret of the fact that he regarded the war as an opportunity to get in a bit of sightseeing. By a stroke of luck he acquired a jeep he nicknamed Lady Chatterley, and a driver named Harry Lackey. Together they followed the Allies as they prepared for D-Day, invaded France, and pushed into Germany.

Dad's pictures from the war are in four formats: six slide carousels that he was happy to show anyone who was interested; 713 prints that generally follow the timeline of the slides; 945 negatives, and 575 large format negatives. I have digitized all of them and selected the best to show here.

Piecing together the story behind these pictures has taken years. Dad's military records were among the 18 million official military personnel files lost in the disastrous July 1972 fire at the United States National Personnel Records Center in St Louis, Missouri. While they have been able to confirm his service and honorable discharge, there are no other records aside from the few he retained.

Dad spoke freely about his adventures during the war but never about the war itself unless asked directly. In later years I offered to help him write his memoirs but he refused. Instead he left his photographs carefully sequenced, labeled, and cataloged. I know that he would like these pictures shared with people who have an interest.

I believe first person narratives are important for the historical record. The stories in this book are written as I remember him telling them, and he and I can share the blame for errors and inconsistencies.

This is what Dad wanted you to see.

Marina Francis Reznor
June 2020

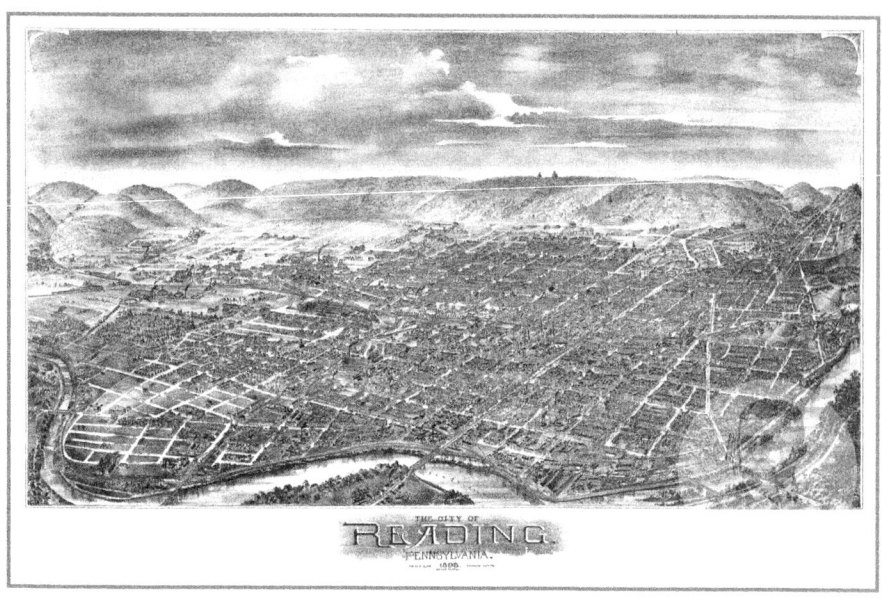

Map of Reading, Pennsylvania, looking east, as it appeared in 1898. The Schuylkill River in the foreground flows southeast to Philadelphia and was a major transportation route to the rich coal regions further inland. The Reading Railroad Company Shops are in the center of town. (Image 1.1)

## Chapter I

## Dad had flat feet

On the afternoon of Sunday, December 7th, 1941 Dad was at his parents' home in Reading, Pennsylvania with his feet up on the sofa, reading a book. He was home from college for the weekend and his father was to drive him back to nearby Kutztown State College after dinner.

His mother came home from visiting down the block and turned on the radio, saying something had happened at a naval base in Hawaii. They listened and heard that the Japanese had attacked Pearl Harbor.

A neighbor knocked on the window. "Wir ziehen in den Krieg," she said. We're going to war.

They both nodded. German was a second language to most residents of Reading.

Three days later Germany declared war on the United States and the United States in turn declared war on Germany. "On Friday I went to the recruiting office to enlist, because I knew I'd be drafted Monday," Dad said later.

Since he was a college senior, Dad's enlistment was delayed until he graduated in May, but they didn't need him on the front lines. Dad was 5ft 4in tall and wore glasses. He also had flat feet, a congenital medical condition called *pes planus*[1]. At that time the military believed *pes planus* made a serviceman unable to march any distance so he failed his physical and was given a 4-F classification—physically unfit for service.

He was 21 years old.


Reading, Pennsylvania, in the early part of the twentieth century was a prosperous city. It was solidly working class and even during the Depression had

---

1   My feet have a very high arch, which is the opposite of pes planus and is called pes cavus.

very low unemployment. The Reading Railroad Company was the biggest employer in town, but it competed with other locally-founded industries for skilled labor. The Berkshire Knitting Mill was the largest stocking factory in the world and Carpenter Steel provided millions of dollars of specialty steel annually to the automobile industry. The cough drop had been invented by Reading-born William H Luden, and he employed more than 1,200 people in his factory at Eighth and Walnut streets.

The industrialists who founded these factories were from Reading, lived in the city, and were generous with their fortunes. They built the Reading Hospital, the Reading Museum, schools, and paid for many civic improvements. In 1927 the city was wealthy enough to build Reading High School at a cost of $1.65 million dollars.

The factory owners were adamant that there be no tenements in Reading, like there were in New York City. A remarkable 60 percent of families lived in houses they owned, and half of those had no mortgage. There was little social unrest, and crime seemed to be restricted to Saturday night bar fights that could involve more than 100 people. Reading was a hard-drinking town and Dad remembered there being a saloon on every corner.

Reading in the early part of the twentieth century was also a remarkably homogeneous city. The population was more than 90 percent white, Protestant, and native-born Americans—by contrast the rest of America was about 72 percent of this demographic. Although there was a good mix of Anglo origin residents like the Francises, the majority were of German descent. These families had initially been attracted by the rich farmland surrounding the city and the easy access to major markets for their produce via the railways. The area still retains its German influence; even today, the local newspaper is interchangeably known as the Adler or the Eagle.

The first Francises came to America in 1682 from Wales, where William Penn had toured to entice skilled workers to immigrate to his colony in the New World. They were blacksmiths, a skill Penn needed in his copper mines west of Philadelphia, and they settled in a small village on the Schuylkill River called Valley Forge.

Penn needed to quickly establish his landholdings in the area. They had been granted in 1680 by King Charles II of England, who was perpetually short on funds. He owed Penn's father, Admiral William Penn, a great deal of money after he had covered the King's gambling debts and Admiral Penn suggested that a large land grant in the New World would be acceptable in lieu of repayment.

The southern border of this grant was the 40th parallel north, but Penn knew that the area just below, on the confluence of the Schuylkill and Delaware Rivers, was the perfect place to establish his capital. Charles Calvert, the third Lord Baltimore, claimed (with ample justification) that the new city Penn called Philadelphia was situated on land chartered to Maryland. He had spent the next 50 years battling William Penn in the British courts for control, which Calvert eventually lost.

Skilled Welsh families flooded into the area west of Philadelphia, which for generations afterwards was called the Welsh Belt. They established farms and businesses, and having no real loyalty to the British Crown fought on the side of American independence. They were amply rewarded when the British surrendered, and in the case of the Francises bought up farms around Valley Forge that had been forfeited by Loyalists.

One hundred years later the Francises moved 30 miles west to Reading, lured by the new railroad. Reading had been founded in 1743 by Penn's two sons who saw the value in a town further up the Schuylkill River at the junction of two fertile valleys, the Lebanon and the Oley. They didn't realize it was also at the southern tip of a remarkably rich vein of hard anthracite coal, which was discovered in 1813. In 1833 the Philadelphia and Reading Railroad was formed to take that coal to Philadelphia where it was loaded onto ships and other rail lines. By 1871 the Reading Railroad was the largest company in the world and probably the first international conglomerate.

At the beginning of the twentieth century Reading had a population of more than 100,000 residents and the Reading Railroad was among the world's most modern and efficient train lines. My great-grandfather was a machinist on the railroad, and he and my great-grandmother had 11 children. The Francis family was solidly working class and owned a new house at 11th and Oley Streets. My great-grandmother was from a large family from nearby

Schuylkill County, and my grandfather, Howard J Francis Sr, remembered 16 or more people regularly sitting down to supper.

After high school my grandfather went to work in the locomotive shop on Sixth Street, called the Reading Company Shops. The Reading Railroad was one of the few in the world that built their own locomotives, and by 1940 my grandfather was the foreman of the diesel locomotive division. He married my grandmother, Blanche, in 1914. She kept her job as a winder in the knitting mill until Dad was born in 1920 because in Reading, everyone worked. There were no other children, and Dad grew up around the extended Francis family and the children of the other railroad machinists.

Tourism in America had blossomed with the spread of railroads at the end of the nineteenth century. By the first decades of the twentieth century, passenger service was well established and the idea of vacations was growing in popularity with the emerging middle class.

Being a railroad town, the citizens of Reading had cheap and easy access to Philadelphia and its many connections. The Francises traveled extensively to New York City, Baltimore, and other attractions. One of Dad's first memories was a family trip to Buffalo, New York in 1927 where they saw Charles Lindbergh fly over the city in his airplane, just after he had become the first person to fly non-stop from New York to Paris.

When I asked Dad many decades later how he knew it was Lindbergh's plane he replied, "There weren't many airplanes in the sky in those days."

# Dad Had Flat Feet

Fleischmann's Yeast enjoyed brisk sales in Reading, Pennsylvania during Prohibition. (Image 2.1)

## Chapter 2

# Ma needs yeast

The Francises weathered the Depression better than most families. An anonymous phone call shortly after the stock market crash of October 1929 suggested they withdraw as much money as they could from the bank, which they did. The Reading Railroad, which had been bankrupted in the Panic of 1893, streamlined their corporate structure and was able to keep people employed but at reduced wages.

Times were tight but Dad, who was nine years old at the time, had already secured a good paying job working for the bootlegger down the street.

Prohibition had been a law since 1920, one year after the Eighteenth Amendment to the United States Constitution had been ratified. Reading barely noticed—the four breweries, five bottling companies, and 25 liquor wholesalers doing business in the city limits continued to operate with healthy profits. The city had a notoriously lackadaisical attitude to the law—in 1923 they were still selling victualers' licenses to taverns—and aside from a few half-hearted crackdowns, the Eighteenth Amendment was lightly enforced.

Its location was key—the surrounding valleys provided excellent corn and hops, artesian well water was plentiful, and the railroad linked the city to a thirsty America. But, by 1925, Reading was getting a reputation as a city where "it was easy to do business", which embarrassed the Federal agents in charge of Prohibition enforcement. They began cracking down on city officials by staging a series of well-publicized raids that netted an enormous amount of illegal alcohol. They also began to scrutinize the sale of the raw ingredients.

Corn, malt, and sugar were easy to get, but the neighborhood bootlegger was forced to hire the local children to procure the cakes of yeast needed for bathtub gin fermentation. They were carefully coached to go to the corner store and slap a quarter on the counter.

"Ma needs yeast."

"But you were just in here yesterday buying yeast."

"Ma needs yeast!"

"Yes, but look, the federal marshals are monitoring how much yeast I sell and—"

"MA NEEDS YEAST!"

Once the cake of yeast was handed over Dad would take it back to the bootlegger and pocket the 15¢ change, or about $8 in today's currency.

Dad was so good at his job that by 1930, when he was ten years old, he was promoted to running the still that made the bathtub gin. The distillation process required close attention and involved several pieces of apparatus, and was Dad's first exposure to chemistry. He liked it and was good at it.

By the time Dad entered high school in 1935, Prohibition had ended and the neighborhood bootlegger had retired. To his regret Dad was forced to "go straight", so an aunt, who was the head housekeeper at St Joseph's Hospital on Walnut Street, got him a summer job helping in the laboratories. St Joseph's Hospital was at the forefront of teaching hospitals and was a pioneer in the use of photography to document cases and treatments. Dad learned photography there.

Dad graduated from Reading High School in 1938 and considered joining the Merchant Marines. His father took him to the physical and Dad returned to the waiting room five minutes after he went in.

"What did the doctor say?" his father asked.

Dad shrugged. "He said 'I have good news and bad news. The good news is you're too tall to be a jockey; the bad news is you're too short to be a Merchant Marine.'"

Instead, Dad enrolled at nearby Kutztown State College. When Germany invaded Poland in 1939, few at the college were surprised. In German class at high school they had listened to recordings of German chancellor Adolf Hitler's public speeches.

"His German was very clear and easy to understand. He was a brilliant orator. After you listened to a few of Hitler's speeches it was obvious what he was going to do."

# Ma Needs Yeast

The Walter Reed General Hospital, home to the US Army Medical Museum, as it appeared in the 1930's. (Image 3.1)

## CHAPTER 3

# Keep your mouth shut, Georgie

Dad graduated from Kutztown State College with a degree in Library Sciences in May 1942 and left for war the first week of June.

Because of his flat feet there was no risk of Dad being sent to an army combat unit. When he reported to Fort Indiantown Gap in Pennsylvania he didn't have to go through basic training but instead was mustered in and sent to the Walter Reed General Hospital in Bethesda, Maryland. He was a Private, First Class, which was the same as a regular Army private but with a bit more pay, $72 a month, to reflect a better education or skill level.

We need to digress a moment and talk about how medical services were organized in the US Army prior to World War II.

In the first year of the American Civil War, a group of wealthy and influential New Yorkers was appalled at the mortality rates of Union soldiers due to unsanitary camp conditions and poor medical services. They banded together and formed the New York Sanitary Commission, which they modeled on the British Sanitary Commission and the work of Florence Nightingale in the Crimean War.

This well-funded and organized group soon began inspecting camps and organizing hospitals. The US Army cooperated with their suggestions and found that the soldiers' health and general condition improved dramatically. The New York Sanitary Commission's influence grew to the point that they were able to pressure Congress and President Lincoln to appoint their choice, 34-year-old Dr William Hammond, as US Army Surgeon General in 1862[2].
Dr Hammond brought needed energy and administrative ability to the mod-

---

[2] The New York Sanitary Commission grew to become the American Red Cross.

ernization of treating war casualties. He standardized the collection of information and specimens from field hospitals and created an Army Medical Museum to study them. This museum quickly evolved into a pathology service that focused on the causes and effects of infectious diseases.

In 1904 the United States started building the Panama Canal, taking over from the French who had failed disastrously when their workforce was decimated by malaria and yellow fever. They turned to the Army Medical Museum to develop a plan to control the spread of mosquito-borne illnesses. The Museum realized that American doctors had no more than a superficial knowledge of tropical infectious diseases or the treatment of heat stroke. Under the direction of Dr Walter Reed, the Museum's curator, it switched its focus to the study of tropical medicine. Dr Reed led the team that proved yellow fever was carried by mosquitoes, which led to a treatment and prevention plan.

During World War I the Army struggled to control the epidemics which spread quickly among the troops. Sanitation in closely quartered conditions was a continuous struggle, and mundane issues of foot ailments and bad teeth began to sideline thousands of otherwise healthy servicemen. And once the troops were in Europe a new problem emerged: venereal disease.

To keep the troops fit to fight, the US Army commissioned the Army Medical Museum to create a program to teach personal hygiene and avoiding temptation. The Fosdick Commission was formed to tackle the problem and, in 1917, created the first government produced educational film, *Fit To Win*. The Army showed the film in training camps and its success prompted the US government to release it to the general public, where it was shown in movie theaters in New York and Pennsylvania. The film, which addressed the issues with unheard of frankness, caused an immediate scandal and under pressure from religious and lay organizations it was withdrawn and the commission disbanded. It was a rare misstep for the Museum.

The Museum's collection of medical artifacts grew quickly, forcing it to move four times in the first 15 years of its existence. Between 1893 and 1910 it also housed the Army Medical School. At the beginning of World War I the Museum was moved to the new army hospital in Bethesda, Maryland just outside of Washington DC, built in 1909 and named after Dr Walter Reed. There the Museum became the center for research on tropical diseases and developed the first typhoid vaccine.

By 1943 the Museum had grown to become the leader in the standardization of diagnosis and the teaching of pathology and disease. The United States had been fighting in the Pacific theater for more than a year, and the Pentagon, which had never fought a protracted war in the tropics, found it needed much more medical support. The Army Institute of Pathology was established, subordinate to the Museum, and organized into four divisions (also called services): Administrative, Professional, Photographic and Medical Arts, and Museum and Medical Arts Services, nicknamed the MAMAS.

The MAMAS were detailed to provide clinical photography and medical illustrations for teaching pathology at the Army Medical School at the Walter Reed, which Army doctors and staff rotated through on short tours of duty. While initially most of their work took place in the surgeries and treatment rooms at the Walter Reed, the MAMAS were organized into small units that could be sent to theaters of war and operate independently.

Each MAMAS unit, or detachment, consisted of an officer from the Sanitary Corps and six enlisted men. Units were dispatched to areas where the Army needed clinical data, particularly on tropical diseases. They photographed patients in treatment and surgical operations, especially neurosurgery and plastic surgery, as well as documenting unusual cases and new techniques. Interesting specimens were shipped back to the Museum for study and research and the pictures they took were used in teaching.

Dad was assigned to the 2nd Medical Detachment, Museum and Medical Arts Service. A friend from St Joseph's Hospital in Reading, which had a teaching relationship with the Walter Reed Hospital, had recommended him for the post. The rest of his group were other 4-Fs with an assortment of conditions, such as diabetes, poor vision, asthma, and bad hearing. Dad also remembered a MAMAS orderly who had been exempted from active service because of terrible acne on his back, which made carrying a backpack difficult.

Dad said his work at the Walter Reed was fascinating and the laboratory facilities world-class. The hospital was also a hub of important military activity that centered on its most famous resident, General John J "Blackjack" Pershing. Until his death in 1948, Pershing was the highest ranking officer in the US military, a position guaranteed by Congress by special authorization in 1919. As such he was senior to all other generals, and military protocol demanded that they pay Pershing a courtesy visit when they were in Washington DC.

Dad said there was a continuous parade of top military brass through the Walter Reed. Blackjack would receive visitors in the main salon of the hospital, and Dad was present the day General George C Patton visited. Pershing, who was 82 years old, had known Patton since they had fought Pancho Villa together in 1917, Patton's first combat experience. General Patton was well-known in the army as a loose cannon who put considerable political stress on his superior officers.

Pershing was curt and got right to the point. "Keep your mouth shut, Georgie. You'll be fine as long as you keep your mouth shut."

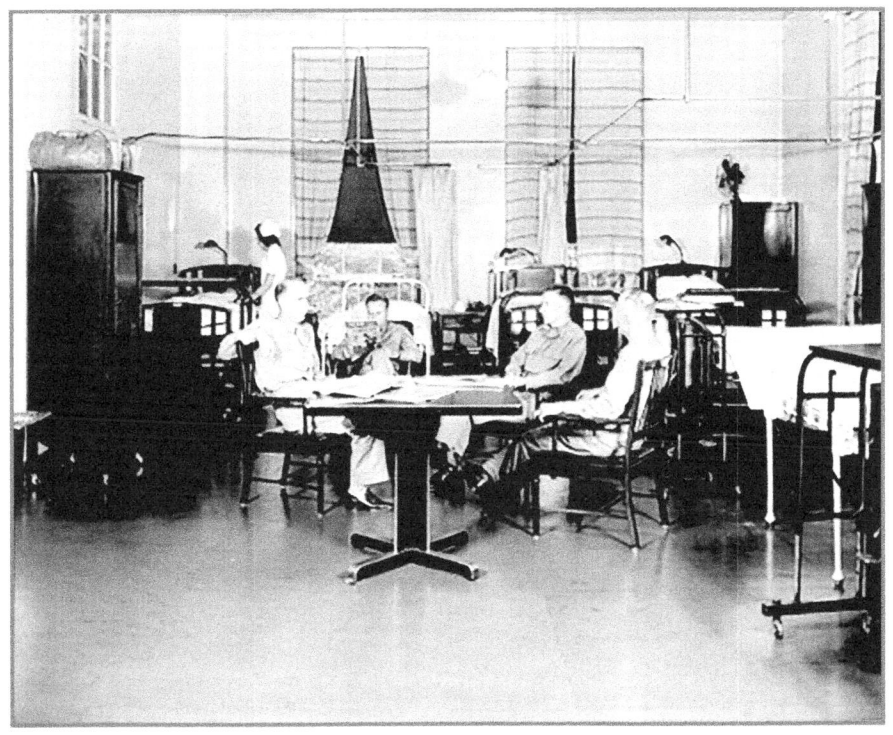

Military patients relaxing in a ward at the Walter Reed Hospital, circa 1942. (Image 3.2)

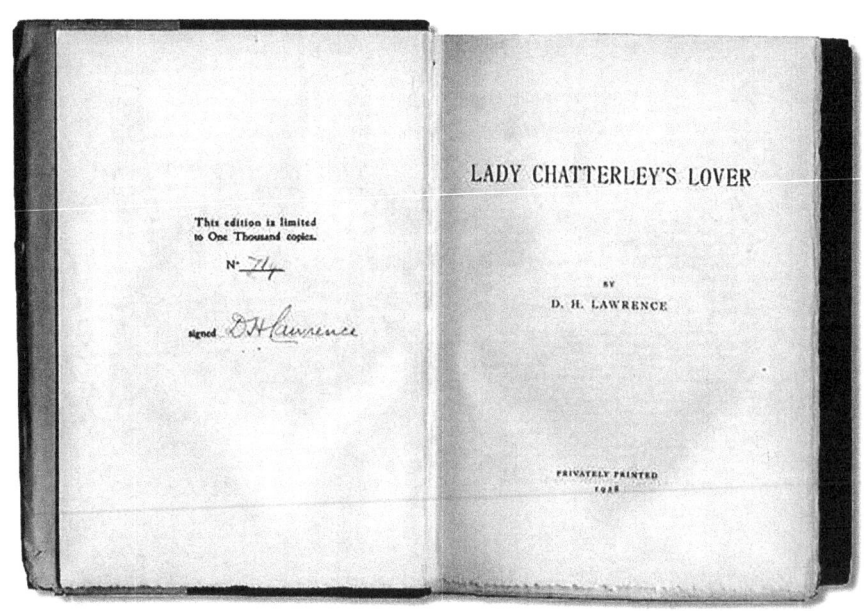

Title page of a first edition of Lady Chatterley's Lover by DH Lawrence, 1928. The book was banned in the United States immediately after publication due to perceived indecency, guaranteeing its popularity. Dad got a pirated copy in college and became a fan. He enjoyed tweaking the nose of prudes and named his jeep after the lead character. (Image 4.1)

## Chapter 4

## *Lady Chatterley*

Labor Day 1943 in the nation's capital was hot and humid, like most late summer days. This was not a surprise, since Washington DC was built on a swamp, an early example of political compromise between the northern and southern states. Air conditioning was unheard of and fans were the only source of cooling.

As the least-senior member of the 2nd Medical Detachment, Museum and Medical Arts Service, Dad was assigned to spend the holiday weekend on duty at the Walter Reed. Everyone else had left the city for the Maryland beaches or the mountains to the west.

As he told it, "I was in the lab when a call came through that the body of a deceased serviceman had been returned from Europe and needed a military escort to his home. I was told to escort the body.

"I had only been in the army two months and had no idea how to go about this. So I went to the Quartermaster's office for more details.

"The sergeant on desk duty took one look at me and cursed. It turned out that the deceased had been a Technical Sergeant, Fifth Class and the military escort needed to be of equal or greater rank. I was a Private, First Class. Since there was no one else to go, I was given an immediate promotion to that rank, which entailed a stack of paperwork.

"The Sergeant then took me through the protocol of escorting the body, emphasizing that I was to make sure the family had transportation to the funeral and home because it was wartime and gasoline was rationed.

"I asked if I should hire a taxi, and his face got red. 'No,' he said, 'you take them in your jeep!'

"I told him I didn't have a jeep.

"He pulled out more forms and slapped them on the desk. 'Then requisition one. And a driver!'

"I was provided with a new uniform and orders for a jeep and driver. The driver was Harry Lackey, a nice guy from New Jersey, and he picked me up in Bethesda and together we drove to Union Station across from the Capitol. Harry supervised loading the coffin onto the train and we began the trip to El Paso, Texas.

"A jeep and hearse were waiting for us in El Paso. We attended the funeral and the family insisted we stay for the get-together afterwards. That night Harry and I got on the train back to Washington DC, and Harry drove us to Bethesda. It had felt cooler in El Paso than in Washington.

"Back at the Walter Reed I went to the desk sergeant to return the jeep and driver. He looked at me like I was crazy. 'Howard,' he said, 'there is one rule in the United States Army and one rule only. When you get something, you never, ever give it back.'"

Dad was now a Technical Sergeant with a jeep, a driver, and an associated bump up in pay. Harry was assigned to the 2nd MAMAS and they nicknamed their permanently requisitioned jeep *Lady Chatterley*. They also discovered that they shared a mutual love of sightseeing.

Their first planned outing, a day trip to Mount Vernon with some nurses, ran into an immediate problem. Gasoline was scarce and it took several ration cards to fill up *Lady Chatterley*. The ration cards were printed by the US government Office of Price Administration on special paper, which was also rationed.

Dad hit upon an ingenious solution. Because the 2nd Medical Detachment, Museum and Medical Arts Service developed and printed pictures that were then used for medical school instruction, they were permitted to requisition paper. Dad requisitioned the paper that the gas ration coupons were printed on, and then photographed a blank ration card which they used to print their own.

Through the winter and spring Dad and Harry enjoyed local sightseeing trips in *Lady Chatterley* until June 1943, when the call came that they were being shipped overseas.

## Lady Chatterley

Motor Ship *Elisabeth Bakke*. (Image 5.1)

## Chapter 5

# The crossing, in which Dad gets his own salmon for dinner

As the 2nd Medical Detachment, Museum and Medical Arts Service prepared to ship out for England, Dad had another important stroke of luck that kept him out of harm's way. Their crossing was scheduled for the end of June 1943.

The Battle of the Atlantic had been won the month before with help from an Enigma Machine that the British Navy recovered from U-Boat, U-559 and deciphered at their code-breaking facility at Bletchley Park. Since 1939 the German Navy had used U-Boats in the Atlantic Ocean with devastating effect, sinking hundreds of ships and killing thousands of merchant marines. These ships were supplying Great Britain's war effort, and Hitler knew that the German Navy's success was jeopardizing British Prime Minister Winston Churchill's ability to continue fighting.

Before the capture of U-559 the outlook for Britain was bleak, but now the British Navy convoy escorts were able to improve their tactics and defeat the "wolf pack" submarines that had preyed on them. The United States was also able to transfer 60 Liberator long-range aircraft from the Pacific to the Atlantic, and sea-scanning radar and depth charges improved. In May 1943, 43 U-Boats were destroyed, including one that carried German Navy Admiral Donitz's son. Shortly thereafter, Donitz recalled the U-Boats from the North Atlantic, leaving the route from North America to Great Britain open.

On June 30th 1943, in New York City, Dad, and the six other members of the 2nd MAMAS boarded the Norwegian merchantman M/s *Elisabeth Bakke*, a 5,450-gross ton motor-ship built in 1937. The *Elisabeth Bakke* had begun crossing the Atlantic earlier in the year; before that she had been shipping freight in the Mediterranean. She saw action in the ill-fated 1942 Operation Vigorous, where the British tried to resupply Malta, an island off of Sicily with strategic importance to the Allies. *Elisabeth Bakke* was part of a convoy (MW-11a) that was forced by the Germans to turn back to the Egyptian port of Alexandria.

Dad's convoy was HX246, code-named "Broom". North Atlantic convoys were organized and run by the Royal Navy, and HX246 was escorted by HMS *Roxborough*, HMS *Deveron*, HMS *Vanquisher*, HMS *Vervian*, HMS *Kingcup*, and HMS *Fressia*. There were 63 ships in the convoy, but only five carried passengers including one troop ship, the *Benjamin Bourne*. *Elisabeth Bakke* carried 12 passengers, Dad's group of seven and five Americans with business in England. The rest carried cargoes of airplanes, fuel oil, kerosene, sugar, and aviation fuel among other items needed in wartime Britain. Commodore RH Mackay, Royal Navy, who was in charge of the convoy, was on board the *Port Adelaide*.

The convoy sailed to Halifax, Nova Scotia where they picked up more ships. On July 5th three escort ships from the Royal Norwegian Navy, the *Acanthus*, *Rose*, and *Potentilla* joined the convoy in St John's, Newfoundland. Dad's group settled into life on board ship, where the accommodation was comfortable and the food excellent.

They got along well with the Norwegian crew, who spoke no English. Dad described them as the biggest and bravest men he had ever met. They, in turn, were perplexed by his small stature, and determined it was because he didn't have enough to eat. One night at dinner the cook brought out a roasted salmon and put it in front of Dad, and then brought out another one for the other eleven passengers. He gained seven pounds on that trip.

They had good sailing weather and saw one iceberg, but the trip was not without mishaps. There was fog and the troop-carrier *Benjamin Bourne* collided with the *Scottish Heather* (a British Admiralty tanker carrying fuel oil) while altering course. On July 9th, a clear day, the *Abner Doubleday* (an American ship carrying tanks) collided with the *JH Senior* (a Panamanian tanker carrying gas and gliders). Commodore Mackay complained that the US ships would not keep proper distance in their columns, which was supposed to be 1,000 yards, but was happier with the US signaling. Overall, however,

## The Crossing, In Which Dad Gets His Own Salmon For Dinner

the Commodore lamented that the American ships were all bad—"slow in answering or repeating a signal, sometimes not repeating at all." The *Frederick Douglass* (American, carrying locomotives and tanks) and *Francis Asbury* (American) were judged the worst.

On July 1st, Commodore Mackay ordered heavy gun practice at a target towed by the HMS *Roxborough*. The Senior Officer of Escort reported afterwards: "Not many customers. The *James E Haviland* had not decoded your signal. The *JH Senior* did a good shoot. The *Richard S Ewell* and all port wing ships were not interested except the *Frederick L Dau*. Port wing ships did not even have guns manned. Total cost: about five tons fuel, one fog buoy ruined, and lower deck cleared to heave in target."

On board the *Elisabeth Bakke*, Dad and his unit relaxed on deck chairs and enjoyed the novelty of their first sea voyage.

On board the M/s *Elisabeth Bakke*, a Norwegian merchant motor-ship, crossing the Atlantic Ocean as part of convoy HX246, code-named "Broom", July 1943. (Image 5.2)

Above: The North Atlantic was a critical seaway in World War II as an armada of vessels ferried American troops and equipment to Great Britain. (Image 5.3) Below: With the threat of attacks from the German Navy still a possibility, this convoy of more than 70 vessels included six Royal Navy and three Royal Norwegian Navy escort ships. (Image 5.4)

## The Crossing, In Which Dad Gets His Own Salmon For Dinner

Above: The ships in Convoy Broom were supposed to travel in tight formation, keeping 1,000 yards apart. (Image 5.5) Below: Howard J Francis Jr, near, and Joe Nale-Povic catch the sun on board the *Elisabeth Bakke*. (Image 5.6)

Above: Three of the five businessmen passengers on their way to Britain. (Image 5.7) Below: Nale-Povic serves a post-dinner coffee to some of the US military passengers in the ship lounge. (Image 5.8)

## The Crossing, In Which Dad Gets His Own Salmon For Dinner

Above: The 2nd MAMAS watch the convoy sail across the North Atlantic. (Image 5.9) Below: Dad described the accommodation on board the *Elisabeth Bakke* (Image 5.10) as comfortable and elegant. As the inset berth card (Image 5.11) shows, Room 6 contained two beds—not bunks—a luxury for most troops.

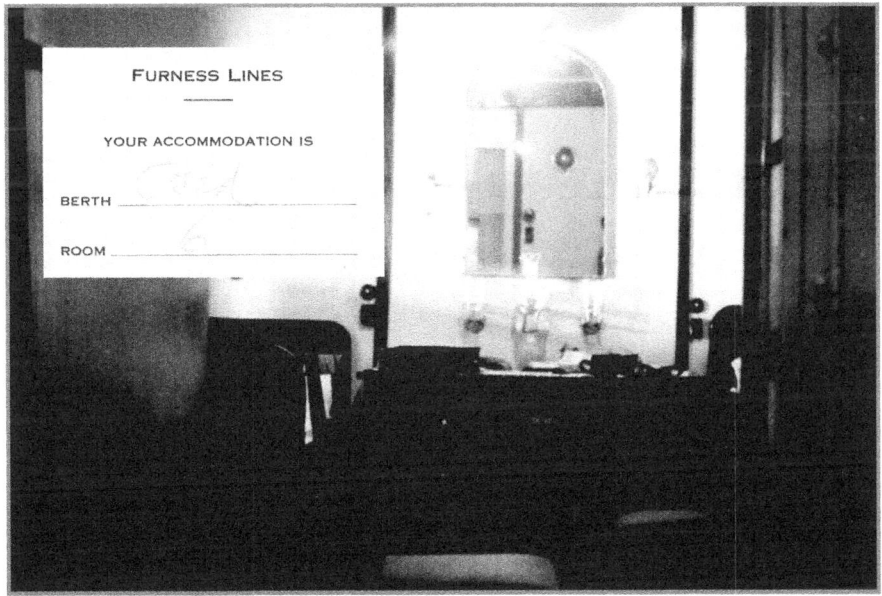

Above: The *Elisabeth Bakke* reached England's north-west at Liverpool on July 14, 1943. (Image 5.12) Below: They sailed along the 40 mile Manchester Ship Canal before docking at Manchester the next day. (Image 5.13)

## The Crossing, In Which Dad Gets His Own Salmon For Dinner

Above: Although too narrow for todays commercial ship traffic, the Manchester Ship Canal was key component for supplying Britain during World War II. This made it a target for enemy bombing, and both Liverpool and Manchester received terrible damage with great loss of civilian life. (Image 5.14) Below: It was an overcast day in Manchester, the light made worse by the smoke coming from nearby factories. (Image 5.15).

A British Army Blood Transfusion Service advanced blood bank sign featuring their vampire bat logo. Western Desert Campaign in Egypt and Libya, October 29 1942. (Image 6.1, © Crown Copyright, IWM)

## Chapter 6

# What you need to know about blood and war

Blood is our main bodily fluid. It is responsible for transporting nutrients, oxygen, carbon dioxide and waste products to and away from cells. An adult who weighs between 150 and 180 pounds (68–82 kilograms) will have about 1.5 gallons (5.7 liters) of blood, of which about half is plasma and half red cells, white cells, and platelets. Plasma keeps the blood vessels from collapsing, and while it helps to maintain blood pressure, it cannot carry oxygen.

The idea of transfusing blood between two people has been around since at least 1616 when British physician William Harvey announced that he had discovered that blood circulates through the body, pumped by the heart. This discovery prompted experiments in transfusion which proceeded for the next 284 years with, shall we say, mixed results.

That is until the beginning of the twentieth century, with the discovery that blood fell into four distinct types. Identification of blood types A, B, AB, and O (which was suspected but not proven to be a blood type that anyone could receive) meant that blood recipients could be matched to donors, an innovation that yielded excellent results. In addition, in 1915 an apparatus was invented that allowed a single technician to perform transfusions instead of a team of doctors and nurses.

During the last two years of World War I, battlefield blood banks were rapidly developed and the United States and Canadian medical army groups pioneered the practice of using recently drawn whole blood for transfusions. Due to the primitive conditions blood-typing was rare and impractical without laboratories. The Canadian Army began using the new transfusion apparatus and, while crude, it saved lives. The evolution of blood transfusion services was one of the most important medical advances derived from World War I, but the problem of preserving drawn whole blood for later use was unsolved.

Another problem was a condition now known as shock. This general term covered conditions that ranged from a drop in blood pressure due to blood loss—now known as hypovolemic shock—to bacterial infections, peritonitis, burns, and pneumonia. World War I experience showed that blood transfusions helped stabilize battle casualties and made surgeries more successful, but they had little effect on the other conditions lumped under the description. A lack of understanding of what actually caused hypovolemic shock and the therapeutic benefit of transfusions delayed treatment with whole blood for decades.

After World War I Major Richard Ohler MC, discovered a direct correlation between blood loss and the degree of shock a patient suffered. At the time there was no way to determine how much blood a casualty had lost, but it was established that transfusing large amounts of whole blood was a very effective treatment.

The Spanish Civil War (1936–39) saw a dramatic improvement in the success of utilizing blood transfusions. This was due to the careful planning and meticulous execution by the Barcelona Blood Transfusion Service, a branch of the Republican Army which maintained a list of donors, prepared more than 27,000 units of blood for forward hospital use, stored it with refrigeration, and kept meticulous records.

At the same time in England, another war with Germany looked almost certain. The War Office created the British Army Blood Supply Depot in Bristol, headed by Brigadier Sir Lionel EH Whitby CVO MC. Whitby, a brilliant pathologist, organized the blood bank system into four districts, each with a central bank from which blood would be sent to military hospitals. This practice was in contrast to the American and German process of bleeding troops at the front lines to provide blood for field hospitals. Whitby also insisted that blood be treated as a perishable and fragile substance, and when war did break out in 1939 this service became invaluable, especially during the heavy German bombing of London in 1940.

## What You Need To Know About Blood And War

The British Army learned from experience with air-raid victims that large volumes of transfusion blood were required. They also discovered that while plasma could restore circulation, only whole blood could make a casualty with a traumatic hemorrhage be fit for surgery. This was an important distinction the United States Army failed to recognize.

Based on this success the British War Office created the British Transfusion Service. Their first battle theater was the North Africa campaign, where they adopted the silhouette of a vampire bat as their logo and set up bleeding stations in tents behind the lines. This allowed surgeons to come forward to where the casualties were and treat them immediately. These doctors, who were used to very limited blood supplies that had to be reserved for the most severe casualties, began to see excellent results when they were able to use whole blood in liberal amounts.

In the United States the first blood bank was established in 1937 at Cook County Hospital in Chicago and featured a modern laboratory to type the blood, preserve it, refrigerate it, and store it. This model quickly spread around the United States and within a few years many community blood banks were established, paving the way for modern surgery.

Advancements in commercial refrigeration helped to increase the length of time whole blood could be stored in specially designed glass vials. But the problem still remained that transfused blood would quickly begin to clot, or get clumpy, and block the tubes in the transfusion apparatus. This was a normal behavior for blood which, by nature, wants to coagulate when exposed to oxygen. After much experimentation it was determined that diluted sodium citrate added to drawn blood greatly reduced coagulation without killing the patient.

This was a key discovery, and by 1938 the shelf life of whole blood was five days. However it still required lab work to type and check for malaria and other diseases, and shipping and storing it in a controlled atmosphere was difficult. Hospitals were able to use it with ease, but bringing whole blood to where it was needed remained a challenge.

A miraculous solution soon appeared when chemist Dr Edwin J Cohn discovered the technique for isolating plasma from blood. Although the existence of plasma had been known since the time of Harvey's discovery, experiments quickly proved that it was an excellent substitute for whole blood in transfusions. Even better, researchers found that any patient could receive plasma regardless of blood type.

Dr Charles R Drew, the first African American to receive a Doctor of Science degree, developed the techniques for preserving plasma and demonstrated its long shelf life and efficacy. Using these techniques, in 1940 he established the "Blood for Britain" program, which collected blood in New York City hospitals and exported it to the United Kingdom to help Blitz victims. Building on the idea of blood banks, he came up with the idea for Bloodmobiles, or trucks with refrigerators that served as blood donation centers.

The success of plasma was astounding. With his Bloodmobiles, Dr Drew demonstrated it could be collected in large amounts, processed in sterile labs, and stored for a long time. It was easy to transport, could be given to any patient, and could even be dried and reconstituted with distilled water[3]. While whole blood had its champions, even they had to admit plasma was a miracle.

When the United States entered World War II in December 1941 doctors were still uncertain that shock was caused by loss of blood volume. British physicians were successfully using whole blood to treat patients who had lost a lot of blood, while American doctors were getting the same results with plasma. The difference was that British physicians were working on bombing victims and battle casualties who needed to be stabilized while waiting for anesthesia and surgery, whereas American surgeons were seeing patients in hospitals under controlled conditions.

That soon changed. In 1942 the United States began to receive battle casualties from the war in the Pacific where plasma, reconstituted from the dry form, became a lifesaving treatment. The war in the Pacific was primarily a naval operation with fighting from island to island, and ships had no trouble producing the distilled water needed to rehydrate dried plasma, which was produced commercially in large quantities in the United States thanks to patriotic blood drives. Even the proponents of whole blood had to concede that

---

[3] Today frozen plasma can be stored for up to 10 years.

plasma was the clear winner in this situation.

The US military soon turned its attention to planning for a land war in Europe. Experience in World War I had taught them that getting supplies to the front lines would be problematic. Estimated casualties were in the tens of thousands and it was obvious there was no way local blood supplies could meet that demand. Dried plasma would need facilities to generate distilled water to rehydrate it and a way to distribute the distilled water to the field hospitals. The War Department began to look into sourcing whole blood in the United States and flying it immediately to bases in England, and from there to the battlefronts in Europe.

An overseas airlift of whole blood had never been attempted. The American Red Cross was brought in to discuss how they transported blood successfully across a wide variety of US climates. The American Society of Refrigeration Engineers was consulted about keeping whole blood between 39 and 43 degrees Fahrenheit (4 and 6 degrees Celsius) during overseas flights and their recommendations were workable. A trial flight of several chests of whole blood was made from New York City to London with encouraging results.

But the War Department soon realized that once the blood reached Europe they had no means of storing it for even a short period of time or the ability to transport it safely over long distances before it became unusable. Whole blood would somehow have to be sourced on the other side of the Atlantic Ocean. But how much, and when would it be needed?

The questions were piling up and there were no good answers, so the War Department turned to Major Robert C Hardin MC, a specialist in blood banking and transfusions from The University of Iowa School of Medicine. In 1942 Major Hardin was appointed commanding officer of the USA European Theatre of Operations Blood Bank, or ETO Blood Bank as it was known.

The choice of Major Hardin was inspired. A brilliant planner who understood the value of using whole blood in the immediate treatment of casualties in shock, Dr Hardin could clearly visualize how the supply of whole blood could work in the European theater of war.

He also understood that the amount of whole blood the US Army would need was being seriously underestimated.

The 2nd Medical Detachment, Museum and Medical Arts Service (2nd MAMAS) with *Lady Chatterley* after their arrival in the summer of 1944 at the 1st Medical General Laboratory, Salisbury England (1st MGL). From left: Harry Lackey, Joe Nale-Povic, Howard Cradick, Ralph Reed, Unknown, Richard "Dick" O'Connell, Howard J Francis Jr. (Image 7.1)

## Chapter 7

# The 2nd MAMAS set up shop

The *Elisabeth Bakke* arrived in Liverpool on Wednesday, July 14th 1943. From there she sailed up the ship canal to Manchester where Dad and the other six men in his detachment disembarked. They took the train to London where they spent a few days sightseeing before reporting to the First Medical General Laboratory in Salisbury, a rural city 90 miles from London and less than 50 miles from the English Channel ports of Portsmouth and Southampton.

The 1st MGL—as it was known—had been built in 1940 as a joint venture between Harvard University and the American Red Cross. Harvard University president James B Conant had been deeply concerned by the 1939 British defeat at Dunkirk and other setbacks, so he contacted the British War Office to ask what needed to be done. The British War Office responded that they needed a hospital that could handle the study and treatment of infectious disease. The American Red Cross was brought in, and the American Red Cross–Harvard Field Hospital was built in Salisbury. Completed in 1941, the hospital had 100 beds and state-of-the-art laboratory facilities.

Almost as soon as it was built the United States entered World War II and the hospital became a US military Medical General Laboratory. In July 1942 Captain (later Colonel) Ralph S Muckenfuss, a distinguished scientist and leading figure in public health laboratory work from Washington University, was put in command. This laboratory service, which was not available in any other theater of the war, proved to be a crucial factor in the outstanding medical service established by the Army in the war in Europe.

The 2nd Medical Detachment, Museum and Medical Arts Service under 1st Lieutenant (later Captain) Ralph D Reed, Sanitary Corps, was attached to the

1st MGL. When they arrived in Salisbury, the hospital was staffed with 39 male officers, 21 nurses, 139 enlisted men, three American civilians, and 68 British civilians.

Rudimentary housing had been set up that Dad said was primitive but comfortable. They were housed in Barrack #2, a long Quonset hut with rows of double bunks and a central coal stove for warmth. Even though they had arrived in summertime, Dad took one look at the small stove and shuddered. He truly disliked the cold.

Fortune smiled again when an enlisted private named Jim from deep in the Appalachian mountains of West Virginia was assigned to their barrack. Dad said he was over six feet, four inches tall and had the constitution of an ox. Jim was one of 12 children and loved army life because there was always plenty to eat. He was used to hard work from sun up to sun down and woke at five o'clock every morning to stoke and fill the coal stove as he had done at home. By the time everyone else woke the barrack was quite warm.

Problems with Jim soon arose. Efforts to keep him busy on the hospital grounds failed because he completed all the work quickly and was ready for more. Seeing the surrounding countryside made him homesick and he began leaving to help the neighboring farmers with their harvest. This was very popular with the farmers who were short of labor, and a policy was eventually worked out that allowed him to be an unpaid "visiting observer", which he enjoyed.

As more US troops began to arrive in England, Dad said it became a big problem keeping them busy as well. Everyone knew there would be an invasion of Europe and it was obvious it wasn't going to happen in winter. The US Army offered classes and training to alleviate the boredom. Dad took a pottery class and became very proficient, as well as a firefighting class.

Dad enjoyed walking out to Stonehenge and Old Sarum, about two miles north of Salisbury. He said it was mostly deserted during the week but was a popular destination on nice weekends. Harry Lackey had arrived with *Lady Chatterley*, but their sightseeing forays were curtailed by travel restrictions and no ability to print their own gas ration coupons in England.

The camp celebrated Christmas and New Year 1944 with a dance, after which the dullness of the English winter set in. The routine was broken in early 1944 when the American boxer Joe Louis visited the 1st MGL. The US War Department sent him on a tour of England to visit American troops and put on some benefit boxing matches. Louis was a worldwide celebrity, having defeated the German champion Max Schmeling to regain the world heavyweight championship title in 1938, a fight that was seen as a battle between democracy and Nazism. He was very popular with all the troops and spent several hours meeting everyone who thronged to see him.

After the visit things went back to their monotonous routine, but by early spring things began to change quickly.

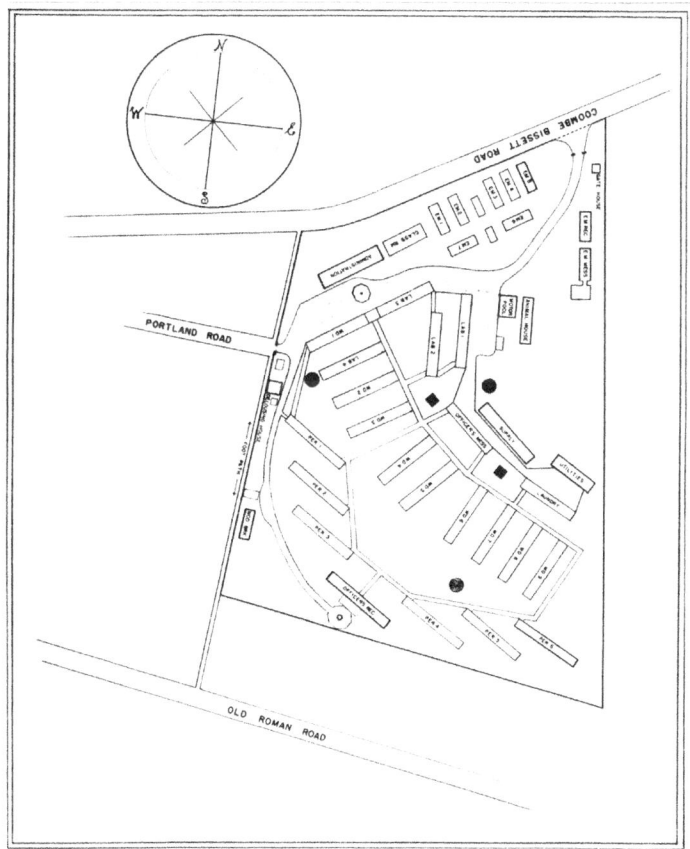

The layout of the 152nd General Hospital and 1st Medical General Laboratory, Salisbury England, 1943. The hospital had been built in 1940 as a joint venture between Harvard University and the American Red Cross. (Image 7.2)

Above: Dad climbed the water tower at the 1st MGL to take detailed pictures of the layout of the facility which were sent back to the Army Medical Museum in Washington DC. He had specific orders and a detail of military police waited for him at the bottom of the ladder. Anyone else attempting this would have been arrested and tried for espionage. (Image 7.3)
Below: Water tower view of the 1st MGL laundry building (with steam rising) and surrounding farm fields. (Image 7.4)

## The 2nd MAMAS Set Up Shop

Above: The 1st MGL administration building. (Image 7.5) Below: Water tower view of Barracks #2, where the 2nd MAMAS were housed. (Image 7.6)

Laboratory facilities at the 1st MGL, where the 2nd MAMAS set up the medical photography unit. Above: Howard Cradick at the lab bench. (7.8)

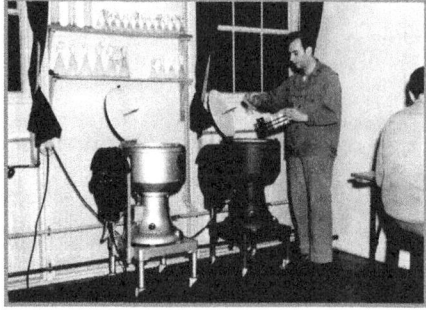

Above: A lab technician with the new laboratory centrifuges (Image 7.9). Left: Howard Cradick and Howard J Francis Jr with a state-of-the-art negative enlarger. The 2nd MAMAS took care to pack all of their equipment themselves and managed its shipping. The US Army's record for delivering sensitive equipment in working order was abysmal. (Image 7.10)

Commanding officers of the 1st Medical General Laboratory and ETO Blood Bank. Above: Chief Nurse Mildred Doane. (Image 7.11) Below: Lt Col Ralph Muckenfuss MC. (Image 7.12)

Above: Lt Kellner, Adjutant 1st MGL. (Image 7.13). Below: Lt Col D Murray Angevine MC, Head of Pathology and Executive Officer 1st MGL. (Image 7.14)

## The 2nd MAMAS Set Up Shop

Salisbury, England. Dad often said the town was the definition of "pastoral". Above: He was fascinated by Salisbury Cathedral, built in the thirteenth century, which remains the tallest spire in the United Kingdom. (Image 7.15)  Below left: the fourteenth-century Poultry Cross, at the junction of Silver Street and Minster Street in Salisbury. (Image 7.16)  Below right: a US Army military parade goes through St Martin's Gate in Salisbury. (Image 7.17)

Dad and the 1st MGL's were able to make several weekend leave trips to London in the late summer and autumn of 1943. Above: Admiralty Arch. (Image 7.18) Below left: the Changing of the Guard at Buckingham Palace. Beginning in 1940 the palace was a frequent bombing target, and the boarded up windows of the palace can be seen in the background. (Image 7.19) Below right: the Red Cross Washington Club in Mayfair, an exclusive part of central London. (Image 7.20)

Above: Howard J Francis Jr and Dick O'Connell, Buckingham Palace. (Image 7.21) Below: The Palm House and Parterre, Kew Gardens in southwest London. After many of the male staff were called up to war in 1940, the women staff ran the gardens. People flocked to Kew to see the demonstration "Victory Gardens". (Image 7.22)

Above: During the late summer and early autumn of 1943 the 2nd MAMAS had time on their hands and *Lady Chatterley* at their disposal. They took the opportunity to sightsee across southern England. Above: Driver Harry Lackey, Ralph Reed, and *Lady Chatterley*. (Image 7.23) Below: The Royal West of England Academy, Bristol, at the time occupied by the US Army. (Image 7.24)

Above: The 2nd MAMAS enjoying a stop at a quaint pond across from a local pub. (Image 7.25) Below: Oxford High Street in the city of Oxford, facing west. (Image 7.26). They also toured the great university's campus, where the perfectly manicured quadrangle lawns made a great impression on Dad.

Above: Stonehenge. The ancient site was an easy walk from Salisbury and a popular weekend destination. Dad said it was usually deserted during the week. (Image 7.27) Below: The rolling Wiltshire countryside outside Salisbury on the way to Stonehenge. (Image 7.28)

# The 2nd MAMAS Set Up Shop

Above: At the beginning of World War II an RAF squadron was formed at nearby Old Sarum. Pilots were in desperate demand and training runs often passed close to Stonehenge. Dad said there were a lot of crashes. (Image 7.29) Below: Sunday afternoon walks to Stonehenge were a popular date. (Image 7.30)

Boredom. Despite having Lady Chatterley for sightseeing excursions, life at the 1st MGL quickly grew monotonous. Above: Troops sunbathing by a chalk foxhole. (Image 7.31)
Below: Dick O'Connell relaxing in Barracks #2. (Image 7.32)

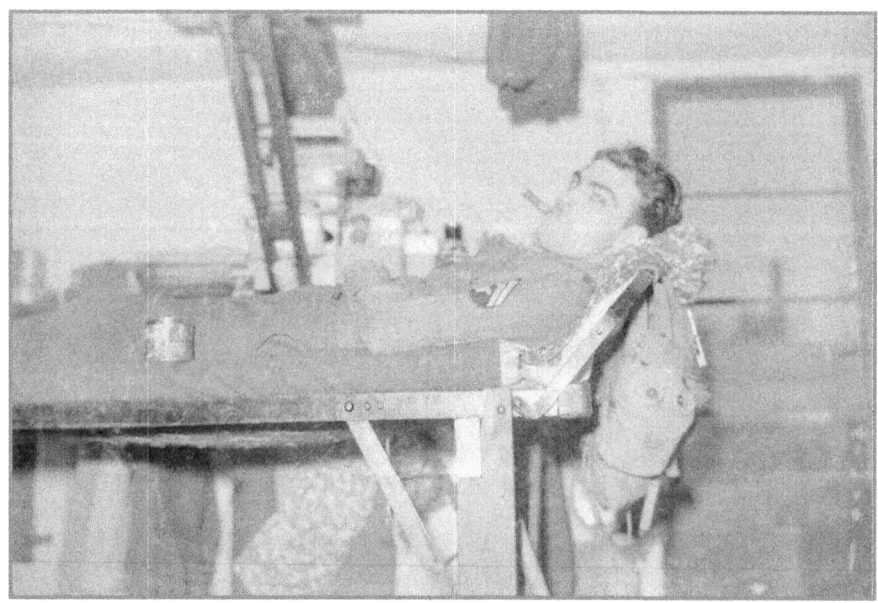

Above: Dad was so desperate for something to do he learned to ride a bike, an activity he never repeated. (Image 7.33) Below: Everyone signed up for a three-day firefighting school offered by the British Army and run by British Army Sergeant Chuttleborough, whose northern English accent was so thick no one could understand a word he said. (Image 7.34)

Christmas and New Year 1943/44 at the 1st MGL. Left: Christmas card from the 2nd MA-MAS. (Image 7.35) Above: The men celebrate in Barrack #2 with a poker game in front of their Christmas tree. (Image 7.36)

Below: New Year's Eve 1943 in Barrack #2. (Image 7.37)

## The 2nd MAMAS Set Up Shop

Above: American boxer Joe Louis, famous for defeating German heavyweight champion Max Schmeling in 1938, visited the 1st MGL in the winter of 1944. (Image 7.38) Below: Louis was touring US Army units in the United Kingdom to keep morale up. (Image 7.39)

Above: The response to Louis' visit was enthusiastic. (Image 7.40) Below: Louis with Lt Col Muckenfuss. Dad said Louis and his staff admitted they were exhausted and overwhelmed by the reception they were receiving all over England. (Image 7.41)

# The 2nd MAMAS Set Up Shop

Private Roy W. Humphrey of Toledo, Ohio is given blood plasma after he was wounded by shrapnel in Sicily on August 9 1943. This famous image demonstrates the technique where one medic could begin a transfusion in the field, where most fatalities occurred from blood loss. (Image 8.1)

## Chapter 8

# Major Hardin's Problems

From the start Major Hardin faced a series of vexing problems, the biggest one being the popularity of plasma. He was one of a minority of doctors who had followed the British wartime surgical outcomes and he was convinced that the red blood cells in whole blood were critical to treating shock. These cells carried oxygen and contributed to total blood mass, which was essential during anesthesia and surgery.

Plasma, on the other hand, lacks this oxygen-carrying capability. It was useful in raising blood pressure after hemorrhage but could not prepare a casualty for major surgery. To confirm this, a US Army doctor was sent to observe the British Army's use of whole blood in North Africa. His conclusions were that while plasma worked well with burns, extreme dehydration, and crushing injuries, it was not a whole blood substitute. He also confirmed that plasma should only be looked on as a first aid measure for dire surgical emergencies and as a supplement for whole blood, not as a substitute for it.

Back in the United States, the Office of the Surgeon General was still solidly in favor of plasma and by 1943 a serious schism had evolved between the whole blood advocates and plasma advocates. Surgeon General Norman T Kirk was among the many doctors who believed that, based on its success in the Pacific, plasma was fine.

The first actual contact the US Army had with the enemy was in July 1943 when the Allies invaded Italy, via Sicily. During the rush of the invasion there was no system for providing and managing blood, but this was quickly corrected and blood began to be flown from the United States to field hospitals in the Mediterranean. An appreciation grew that giving whole blood, and a lot of it, to battle casualties produced excellent results.

Major Hardin knew that the European theater of operations would be very different from the Mediterranean, where a single army operated on a single landmass in a limited area. Delivery of blood in Italy, while challenging, was never hampered by flying over water in bad weather. In Italy, medical control could be uniform because there was a single army and a single army surgeon. If things went well for the Allies after they invaded Europe, there would be five US field armies, each with their own surgeon and separated by very rough terrain.

In November 1943 Surgeon General Kirk was given a proposal to include preserved whole blood in the transatlantic airlift that was being planned for the invasion. The estimated amount of blood to be transported was huge and the Surgeon General rejected the proposal. He felt the logistics of the operation were insurmountable.

General Paul Ramsey Hawley, Command Surgeon of the European Theater of Operations, concurred with this opinion. It was learned after the war that the decision not to include whole blood in the transatlantic airlift had been made by General Hawley the previous July. Both generals knew that there were more important priorities for the scarce cargo space in the airplanes, and plasma was an excellent alternative that could be sent by ship.

With no whole blood coming from the United States it was obvious Major Hardin would have to secure whole blood locally. And he would have to do so without disrupting the well-organized British Army Transfusion Service led by Brigadier Whitby (who providently had a very good relationship with the US military leadership that needed to be preserved). They would establish a reservoir of O type blood donors in Great Britain who were under US military control and modeled on the British Army Transfusion Service, which was having so much success in North Africa.

Next, Major Hardin decided to create from scratch a blood bank that would provide an adequate supply of blood, at least for the initial phases of the invasion. This would require skilled personnel to collect blood, laboratory facilities to type and check for diseases, and a secure storage area.

# Major Hardin's Problems

Most importantly, this new blood bank needed to be close, but not too close, to the English Channel.

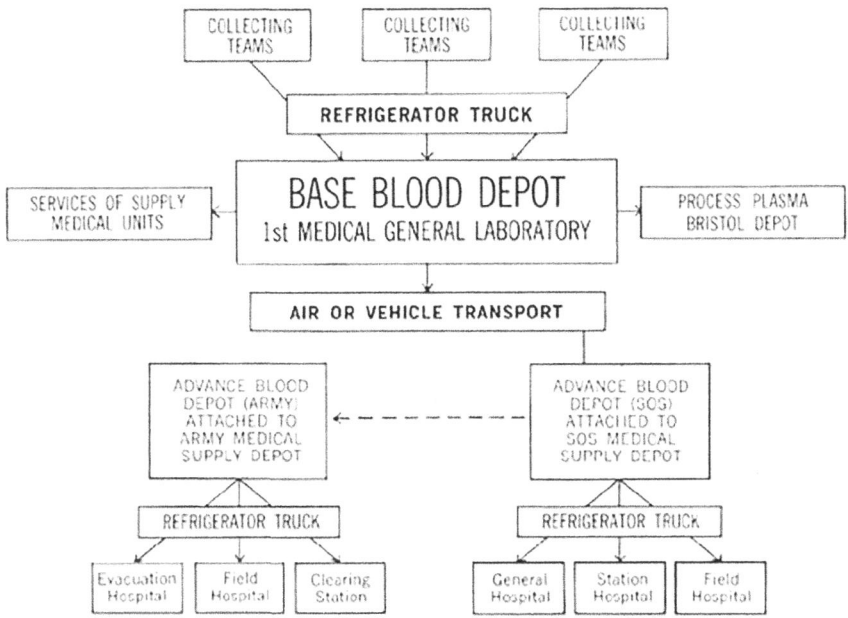

The flowchart Major Hardin and his team created to lay out the plan for supplying whole blood to the front lines in France immediately after the invasion in June, 1944. (Image 8.2)

Decoding a World War II US Army service tag, style #1, issued between November 1941 and July 1943: Name, Army serial number, tetanus dates (1942 and 1943), blood type (A), and next of kin. There was no technology to test for positive or negative Rhesus factor at the time. If a service person had a religious preference for burial it was marked in the bottom right corner - C (Catholic), P (Protestant), H (Hebrew). This practice was stopped when it was learned captured Jewish solders were being executed by the Germans based on their religion. Above: Dad's dog tags. (Image 9.1)

## Chapter 9

# The Meeting at Salisbury

Major Hardin put his plans to create a blood bank into action quickly. Since there was no US Army medical department unit that could do this job, an entirely new organization was created. It would have 11 officers and 143 enlisted men, and would be attached for rations to nearby organizations.

By January 1944 it was decided that the 152nd Station Hospital in Bath—40 miles northwest of Salisbury—would staff the European Theater of Operations Blood Bank (ETO Blood Bank) and that 1st Medical General Laboratory was the perfect location. On January 22nd the 152nd Station Hospital was moved to Salisbury and attached to the 1st MGL. Colonel Muckenfuss was made commanding officer of both units, which for all intents and purposes operated as one. Major Hardin became the Executive Officer of the blood bank.

Almost all of the hospital staff was moved out and staff who knew how to draw and handle blood were brought in. Surgical technicians were trained to collect blood and 16 enlisted men were trained to clean, assemble, and sterilize equipment. Dad and the 2nd MAMAS were in charge of processing the blood in the laboratory, which was equipped with state-of-the-art centrifuges and microscopes.

One highly-sought after staff person was the refrigerator mechanic, who played an essential role in the operation of a blood bank. Commercial refrigerators had been in use since World War I, and the first refrigerator truck was introduced in 1925. Featuring a roof-mounted mechanical refrigeration system pioneered by Frederick Jones, these insulated vans were primitive and the jostling from rough roads caused frequent breakdowns. Specially trained mechanics had to travel to the stranded trucks with all their tools and replacement parts, as well as canisters of replacement Freon gas. The theater of war was combed for these mechanics and, eventually, enough—24—were recruited, along with 60 truck drivers who were trained to transport refrigerated blood.

By February 1944 all of the personnel of the 152nd Station Hospitals were there to meet the needs of the blood bank. They were divided into four mobile collection teams, each made up of seven enlisted men (including a driver) and one medical officer. Each team could draw blood from an average of 20 men in an hour and up to 150 people a day.

Major Hardin rejected using British civilians as volunteer donors for the ETO Blood Bank early in the planning because no one wanted to interrupt the operation of the British blood bank. The decision was made to use only US military volunteers with O type blood and 473 milliliters—slightly more than the one pint donors give today—would be drawn at each collection. It was clearly stipulated that no one could donate more frequently than every 90 days. And, although donors had been paid $10 in Italy, General Hawley decreed that no donors would be paid in Great Britain.

By early spring 1944 US troops were stationed in camps of every size scattered all over the United Kingdom. Units were instructed to prepare a list of volunteer O-type donors, and Major General Lee, Commander of Services and Supply, sent a message to the troops encouraging them to volunteer. "You, who are eligible, may well be proud of this opportunity to place your name on this roll of honor. – the Blood Panel, European Theater of Operations".

The ETO Blood Bank was ready for business. Two questions remained: how much blood would be required and when would it be needed? Major Hardin had his answer soon after, when he was ordered to report to General Hawley's London headquarters. Inside, Hawley's aide, Colonel Liston took him to the middle of a large room and the date of D-Day was whispered in his ear.

A caveat was added that this was a planning date and that the actual invasion, code named Operation Overlord, would occur within 48 hours of that date. Major Hardin never wrote down this date or told another soul, but he now knew when he had to begin collecting blood in earnest and when that blood needed to be moved to the English Channel.

On April 1st 1944 a meeting was held at the 1st MGL to finalize the plan to supply whole blood for the invasion. Surgeon General Kirk, visiting from America, attended. The most pressing order of business was to calculate the amount of blood needed.

Original estimates, based on the British Blood Transfusion Service, indicated that a ratio of one pint of whole blood for each ten casualties would be adequate. But at the meeting, Colonel Thomas J Hartfort MC, Office of the Surgeon, related that he had just returned from Italy where a supply of one pint of whole blood was now considered necessary for every 2.2 casualties rather than the ten originally estimated (four and a half times more).

Operation Overlord estimated casualties on the Continent would be an average of 1,875 per day, which would mean that, allowing 250 cc (8.5 fluid ounces) of blood for each casualty in shock (estimated at 20 percent of the total number of casualties), 200 pints of blood per day would be required. Operation Overlord was planned for 90 days, so 18,000 pints would be required with a maximum peak of 600 pints per day for shorter periods. There was storage space for 3,000 pints of blood at the 1st MGL and the blood could be stored for a maximum period of 14 days before being sent to the continent.

This increased demand seemed so far out of reach with the available sources—who, remember, were not allowed to be paid—that once again flying whole blood from the United States seemed like the only solution. If not, it was calculated that 90 percent of all O-type US military personnel in Great Britain would have to donate.

The top-secret meeting at 1st MGL, April 1st 1944. Many of the senior US Army medical staff planning Operation Overlord were experienced surgeons, a convenient fact when 80% of the casualties needed surgical attention. Above: 2nd MAMAS Capt Ralph Reed (left) greets US Surgeon General Norman T Kirk (center), escorted by Lt Col Muckenfuss. (Image 9.2) Below, left to right: Unidentified two-star US Army general, Col David E Liston, MC Deputy Chief Surgeon, European Theater of Operations, Lt Col Ralph S Muckenfuss. (Image 9.3)

Above, far right: US Army General Paul Ramsey Hawley, Command Surgeon of the European Theater of Operations preparations for D-Day. (Image 9.4) Below, front, left to right: General Hawley, Surgeon General Kirk, Lt Col Muckenfuss, Col Liston. (Image 9.5)

TIME Magazine, 1944. It was estimated that during World War II one in five Americans looked at a TIME Magazine or sister publication Life Magazine at least once a week. (Image 10.1, collection of the author)

## Chapter 10

# Who the hell let *TIME* magazine in the door?

After the April 1st meeting it was time for the teams to begin collecting blood. Appearances were key—any unusual activity at the ETO Blood Bank would be a clear indication the date of the invasion was approaching. It was also a classified secret that advances in refrigeration and anticoagulants had increased the shelf life of whole blood to 21 days.

Major Hardin hit on a plan that would make it appear the blood bank had been "turned on", or was collecting in preparation for the invasion. Hectic activity at the main blood bank in Salisbury was choreographed to produce confusion among observers, and collection teams were sent far away and always to units where there were too few donors to be of significance when blood needed to be drawn in earnest.

Dad was a team member tasked with blood typing and testing on the road. He enjoyed traveling around Great Britain but said even he was surprised at the very out-of-the-way places they were sent. From his pictures we know they went to Scotland, Wales, and Northern Ireland with plenty of time for sightseeing after a collection visit.

According to Dad, the process went like this: the blood-drawing team would arrive at a US military base where a large tent in a quiet area of camp had been prepared for them. Long tables would be set up at the entrance and staffed by base personnel. Behind them a series of portable screens shielded most activity, or lack of it.

The blood collection team worked quickly and efficiently. All volunteers—regardless of blood type—were taken behind the screens for an examination, where almost all were deemed ineligible for some reason. They were then moved to several screened waiting areas before being dismissed. A few A, B, and AB blood-type donors were bled in full view of the waiting areas and at the end of the day those few donations were rushed in clearly marked 500-pint refrigerators to the ETO Blood Bank in Salisbury.

From a distance the teams gave every appearance that they were drawing a considerable quantity of blood. The collected blood was distributed to local hospitals so that there was no evidence at the 1st MGL of how little blood was actually being stored.

Several weeks went by and even though the teams were rejecting almost all volunteers, the response to the request for donors was disappointing. It had been agreed that no combat unit should donate later than 60 days before it was expected to go into action, but infantry leaders were reluctant to allow their troops to volunteer, fearing they would be left weak and not fit for duty despite reassurances otherwise. Able-bodied American troops were pouring into England by the thousands yet less than 20 percent volunteered. General Hawley again rejected the idea of paying donors, but arranged several perks, like extra candy or cigarettes. Even so, response remained low.

On May 1st 1944 it was brought to General Hawley's attention that the April 24th edition of *TIME* magazine had run an article about the ETO Blood Bank in Salisbury.

*TIME* magazine, April 24 1944 – Medicine: Blood for Invasion

Last week in England, as for several weeks past, the U.S. Army's Major Robert Hardin carried out what he calls a "dry run" of blood-giving. Soldiers with type-o blood (the universal type which can be given to anybody) gave four-fifths pint each to his blood banks — in this case, refrigerator trucks.

Patriotic donors at home could rest assured that blood plasma, which is blood with the red corpuscles removed, is often a lifesaver. But a really bad hemorrhage produces a dangerous reduction in red corpuscles, which carry oxygen to the tissues. Though a man can get along on less than half the ideal number of red corpuscles, he may die from lack of oxygen in his tissues if the shortage gets acute.

As last week's dry run was just for practice, much of the blood went to the American hospitals where blood is nice to have — whole blood is the best of all pick-me-ups for a weak patient — but not really needed. If unused for 20 days or so, the blood is thrown away; by then the corpuscles begin to die.

Some three weeks before invasion, the dry runs will become "wet". The Army will then begin drawing on its soldier donors for a bank of whole blood to be used on the beachheads and in the foxholes of Europe.

The *TIME* magazine article was uncomfortably accurate and General Hawley was livid. He said: "After such an announcement, no better indication could be given to the enemy of the date of the impending invasion that the start of a stepped-up collection of blood." Who the hell had let *TIME* magazine in the door?

Colonel Muckenfuss said no correspondent had visited the 1st MGL. He had no idea of Major Hardin's timeline. The term "dry run" was not being used.

Major Hardin admitted that several months before D-day he had been visited by an Army public relations officer who had a *TIME* reporter in tow. The reporter had casually asked how long blood could be kept? Major Hardin let slip the proper answer was 21 days, and the reporter correctly assumed that blood would start to be drawn in earnest 20 days before the invasion. That assumption was uncomfortably correct.

In late April the ETO Blood Bank got an opportunity to test its process.

Exercise Tiger was a dress rehearsal for D-day, five weeks before the planned invasion. On April 28th a practice assault was organized on the Dorset coast at Slapton Sands to acclimate troops to real battle conditions. Several landing ships were loaded with troops and set into the English Channel, and disaster struck when a German U-Boat convoy off Portland discovered them and opened fire. Two LSTs—Landing Ship, Tank—were sunk and two made it back to shore. There was so much confusion and so many incidents of friendly fire on shore that D-Day was almost canceled. Reports vary, but upwards of 946 men lost their lives, more than were killed at the actual landing at Utah Beach.

Casualties were hospitalized at nearby US Army field hospitals and the ETO Blood Bank was called on to supply the large amounts of blood needed. The blood bank worked smoothly. As a result of the disaster, several changes came about before D-Day, including standardizing the radio frequencies between the ships and life-vest training for the troops. Survivors were sworn to secrecy and the Army and Navy made the information about Exercise Tiger top-secret for years after the war ended.

Spring 1944. The blood-drawing teams were sent out from Salisbury to the most far-flung US Army camps in Great Britain. While the teams simulated a great deal of activity at the blood donation stations, they had time to do some sightseeing before and after. Below: Bournemouth, on England's south coast. (Image 10.2)

Above: Dower House in Bristol, the largest city in England's West Country, built from sandstone. It has multiple nicknames, including Custard Castle and Sand Castle. (Image 10.3)
Below: The Parade Ground, Edinburgh Castle, Scotland. (Image 10.4)

Above: Carrickfergus sea front, Northern Ireland. (Image 10.5) Below: A US Army field hospital near Plymouth, May 1944. The date and proximity to Slapton Sands would suggest that these patients were survivors of the Exercise Tiger disaster. (Image 10.6)

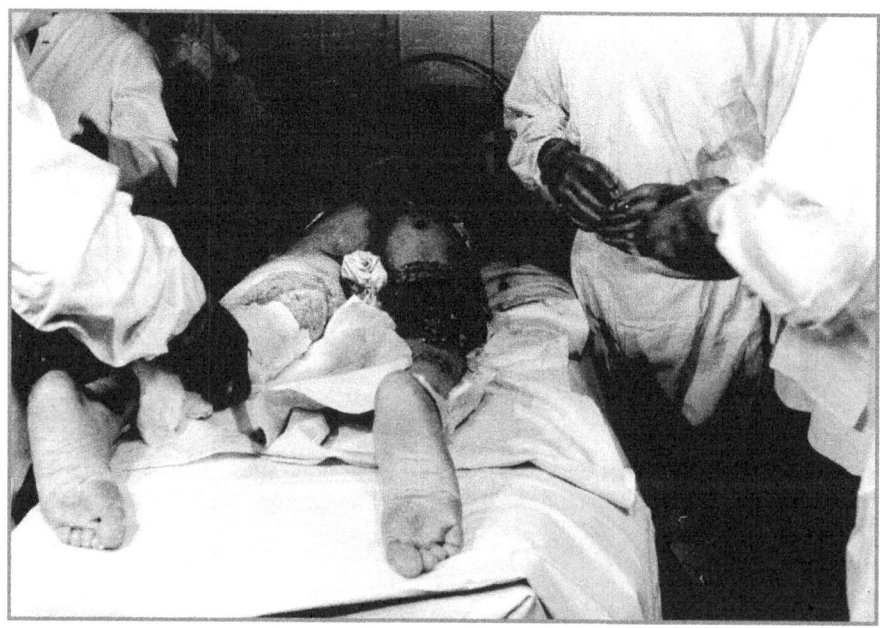

# Who The Hell Let TIME Magazine In The Door?

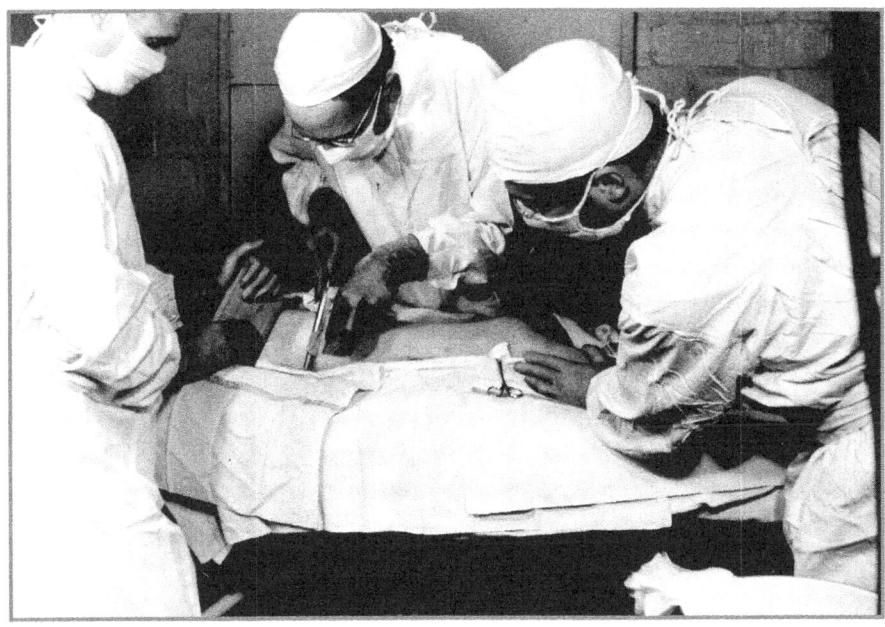

Above: One of the duties of the 2nd MAMAS was to document US Army field hospital surgical procedures. Here a surgeon begins an amputation. (Image 10.7) Below: The US Army field hospital in Plymouth. The Exercise Tiger disaster was the first test the US Army Medical units had in the United Kingdom before D-Day. (Image 10.8)

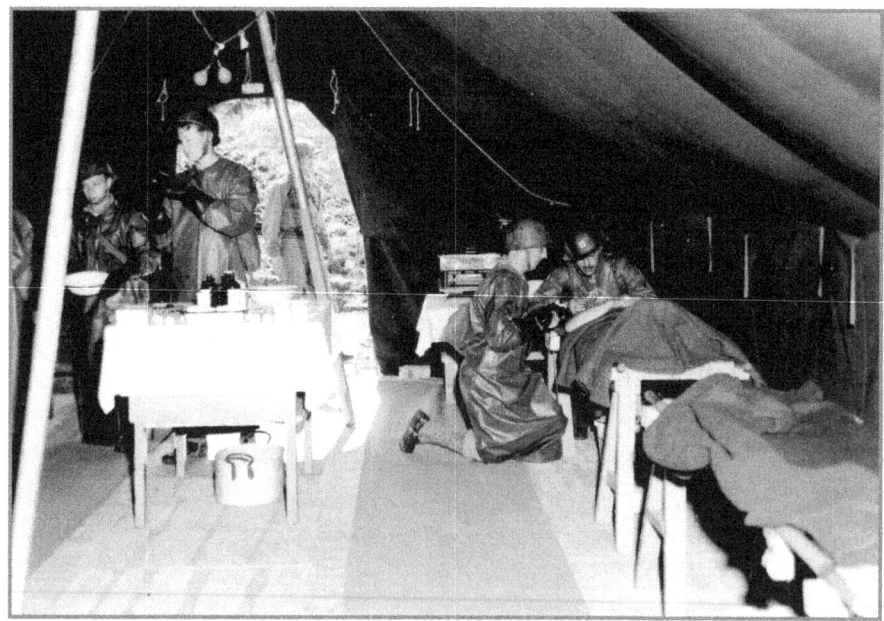

Above: Wounded in tents near Plymouth, May 1944. (Image 10.9)  Below: It was easier and faster to treat the injured on a train than in an ambulance or on a truck. As a result, a number of trains were converted into mobile hospitals, where doctors and nurses could give earlier treatment to the severely before they reached better-equipped hospitals. Here a medic treats a severely injured man. (Image 10.10)

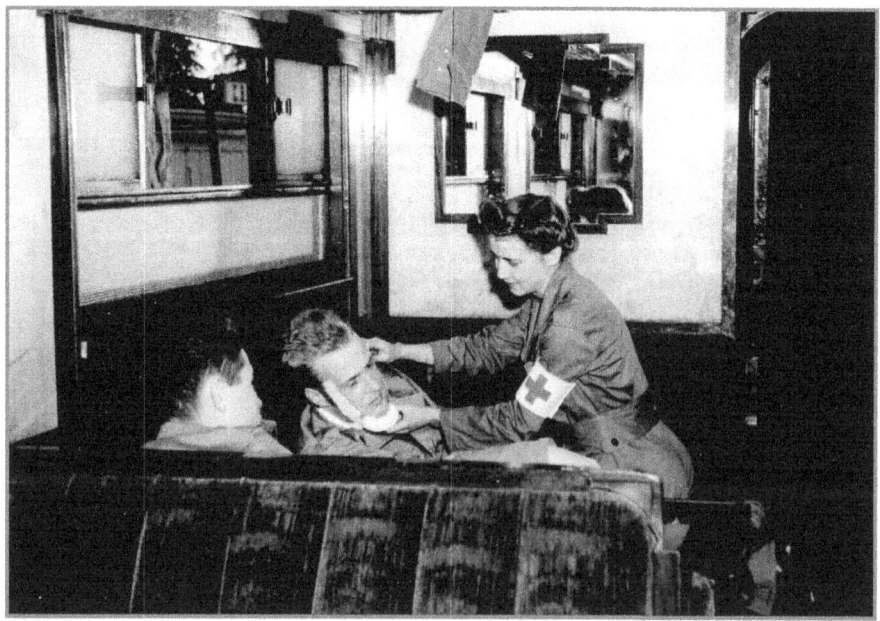

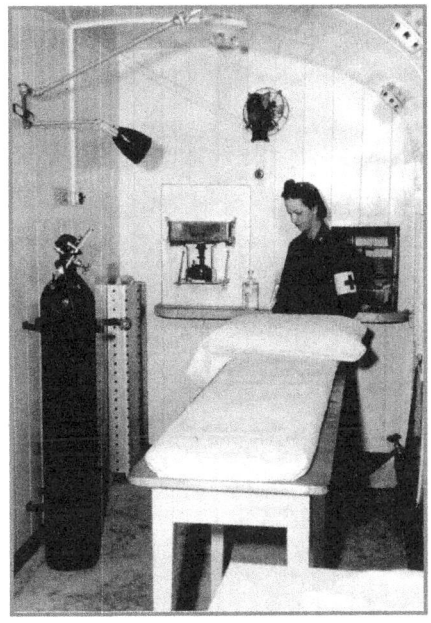

Above: A nurse prepares an operating theater on a US Army hospital train. (Image 10.11)
Below: A medic treats a soldier with head injuries. (Image 10.12)

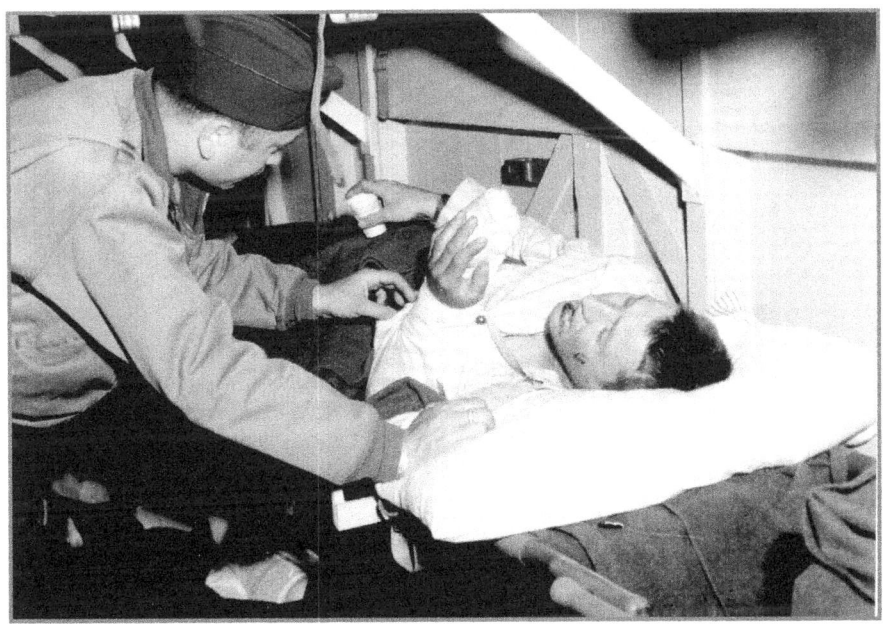

Shipping canisters used by the ETO Blood Bank. These zinc-lined insulated cans, nicknamed "Mermites", were packed with ice and filled with up to 20 flasks of whole blood. (Image 11.1)

## Chapter 11

# Blood begins to flow

On May 23rd, 1944 Major Hardin turned the ETO Blood Bank in Salisbury on.

Dad said they knew D-day was approaching because suddenly the blood-drawing teams were sent locally to huge bases in the south of England where they hadn't been before. They collected blood from everyone and worked from before sunrise to after sundown.

Dad had huge admiration for the Army nurses who drew the blood. He would laugh when he remembered that the largest and brawniest volunteers were the ones who usually fainted. The nurses would direct the orderlies to lay them on the ground saying, "No one's ever fallen off the floor", and they'd collect blood from them there.

In mid-May Major Hardin had been called to the British Naval Headquarters in Southampton and was given the secret locations and times that the invasion ships would dock and be loaded in the coastal ports. He never wrote the information down and he was the only one who knew. On June 1st, he personally supervised the loading of the refrigerator trucks in Salisbury and drove with them to the coast. The drivers had no instructions and didn't know where they were going.

He had sent members of his staff to each of the embarkation ports to meet the drivers and bring them behind the barbed wire, where they were kept until the invasion. From June 1st to June 3rd, 109 LSTs—each with ten pints of blood—were loaded at seven embarkation ports along the coast.

Operation Overlord commenced on June 6th 1944. American troops landed across the Channel on Normandy beaches code-named Utah and Omaha, the British at Gold and Sword, and the Canadians at Juno. German units stationed on that section of the French coast mounted a punishing defense but received no reinforcements or clear instructions from their German superior officers, who were either away on holiday (Rommel had gone home to celebrate his wife's birthday) or taking part in war games elsewhere. Hitler had left orders he was not to be woken under any circumstances and it wasn't until two o'clock in the afternoon that he learned of the invasion.

On the afternoon of D-Day the Allies began building two artificial ports on the Normandy shore, called Mulberry Harbors, to begin receiving the tons of supplies they needed to continue fighting. Hitler had correctly predicted that no force could invade France without control of a major harbor on the English Channel, but he never dreamed such a harbor could be manufactured. The first, at Gold Beach near Arromanches, operated for ten months after D-Day and landed more than four million tons of supplies. The second, at Omaha Beach, was destroyed by a violent storm 13 days after D-Day but the beach was still accessible to LSTs and the Americans were able to unload millions of tons of supplies.

When I asked Dad, years later, if he had gone across on D-Day he replied, "Yes, many times." All medical personnel were on hand to deal with the casualties and Dad was assigned to an LST. He never said which one, but remarked he was surprised at the amount of jellyfish in the water on the Normandy side.

The original plan was to provide 1,000 pints of whole blood between D-Day and the following five days. The blood, once delivered, would be sent as far forward as the field hospitals in refrigerator trucks. A transfusion officer in each unit would be responsible for maintaining an adequate supply of blood. The first blood depot was set up at Omaha Beach on June 7th, where a Navy-type refrigerator was buried in the sand and eight trucks delivered 80 pints each to field operations. Back in the English ports, blood from the ETO Blood Bank was continuously loaded on the LST's which were ferrying wounded troops back from the front lines. Very little blood was wasted.

On June 9th two refrigerator trucks were landed on Utah Beach and by June 12th they had set up a blood distribution and medical supply depot nicknamed Martha Dump. The trucks of this detachment could readily distribute all the whole blood available to nearby field and evacuation hospitals.

## Blood Begins To Flow

By June 13th an emergency airstrip had been built close to Omaha Beach and blood from the ETO Blood Bank began to arrive by air. Following this, C-47 planes brought in practically all blood from the United Kingdom, along with ether and penicillin. The C-47s then evacuated casualties to the 217th General Hospital at Swindon via Membury Field airbase, 40 miles directly north of Salisbury.

Due to the success of counter-intelligence operations, Hitler still expected the main Allied invasion to be further west in the Calais area and for weeks forbade his generals from moving troops east to Normandy. The real number of casualties was much lower than the pre-invasion planning estimates, and by Day 44 of the invasion 15,250 pints of blood had been delivered for 46,918 casualties, a ratio of one pint for every three wounded. Casualties who needed blood were 56 percent below the estimate and the whole blood supply from the ETO Blood Bank was considered reasonably adequate.

Data soon became clear, however, that the magnitude of blood loss sustained by casualties in severe shock was much greater than expected. Reports also showed that field hospitals were not using whole blood extravagantly, and that it was not only saving lives but making recovery faster. By mid-July the ETO Blood Bank was supplying 500 pints of whole blood daily to the European mainland and utilizing its donors to full capacity. Dad remembered this as a time that anyone and everyone was being bled, sometimes as often as once a week. Even though he was Type A, Dad gave blood often. The labs at the 1st MGL were running 24 hours a day to type all blood drawn and get it across the Channel as quickly as possible.

By the end of July, after sustained bombing, the Allies broke through German resistance at St-Lô and the demand for blood began to far outpace the supply. One problem was that whole blood was being used by shock teams to prepare patients for surgery, but those patients became backlogged as more severe cases came in. They needed the whole blood to remain prepped for surgery, a situation not taken into consideration in planning. Demand was now 1,000 pints per day, while the US service donors in the United Kingdom could, at most, produce 400 pints daily (an additional 250 pints sourced from Air Force personnel was considered temporary). There was no ability to make up the remaining 350 pints, nor to address the anticipated increase in demand of up to 550 pints daily when the US Third Army became operational in August. General Hawley immediately issued a command that whole blood would be airlifted from the United States to Prestwick, Scotland, and from there on to mainland Europe. The Red Cross set up blood donor centers in Boston, New York, and Washington DC. There was a test flight on August 21st from New York City to Prestwick, where the blood was then taken by refrigerated truck to Salisbury (a road journey of around 450 miles, taking almost 11 hours), and then flown to France, where it arrived 27th August 1944.

D-Day casualties were first treated in field hospitals near the front lines in France and then transfered back to Great Britain. Those in greatest need were evacuated by aircraft. Below: Air evacuation of casualties landing at Membury Airfield, near Swindon. (Image 11.2)

Above: Medics at Membury Field waiting to transport the injured to nearby hospitals. (Image 11.3); Below: A flight lands after another successful mission. (Image 11.4)

Above: An injured soldier is taken from the plane on a stretcher to a waiting ambulance. (Image 11.5)
In the first few days of Operation Overlord, invasion ships returned with hundreds of evacuated casualties. Below: Four invasion ships berthed in Weymouth Harbour. (Image 11.6)

# Blood Begins To Flow

Above: Boats of all sizes were utilized for the invasion and to return the injured to England's South Coast. (Image 11.7) Below: Armed vehicles sit in protection of the vessels as the injured are off-loaded. (Image 11.8)

Above: Ambulances ready to receive the wounded. (Image 11.9) Below: US Landing Craft Tank Mary (217) arrives at Weymouth Harbour. (Image 11.10)

# Blood Begins To Flow

Above: More than 50 wounded servicemen lie on the deck as their vessel reaches the safety of England. (Image 11.11) Below: Troops waiting for the all clear before they can go off to the hospital for treatment. (Image 11.12)

Above: Walking wounded disembark next to USS LST 325, which was launched from Philadelphia Naval Shipyard in October 1942 and took part in the first wave of Normandy landings before making 40 trips across the English Channel. (Image 11.13) Below: Conditions in the hold of an LST returning wounded to Weymouth Harbour. (Image 11.14)

Above: Stretcher-borne injured were at the greatest risk, not only from infections in their wounds, but also given the difficulty of moving them. (Image 11.15) Below: Other vessels allowed for exit through a lowered bow end. (Image 11.16)

Dad fishing in the Sarthe River off the École Normale, headquarters of the 10th Medical Laboratory and 2nd MAMAS, Alençon, August 1944. (Image 12.1)

## Chapter 12

## "Everyone speaks French here. Even the little kids."

In August 1944 the Allied armies advanced through France and began to press on German-occupied Paris. Field hospitals needed laboratory services so the 2nd Medical Detachment, Museum and Medical Arts Service in Salisbury were given orders to pack up their supplies and cross the Channel. They reached Utah Beach in mid-August.

Harry Lackey and *Lady Chatterley* followed Dad across the Channel. Churchill, in his six-volume history of World War II, noted his intense displeasure at the amount of equipment that the Americans were shipping to the continent from England, including thousands of what Churchill viewed as unneeded jeeps. It's not known if the Prime Minister was aware that Ford Motor Corporation had calculated the life expectancy of a Jeep in combat to be less than 90 days.

Harry had never been anywhere that English was not spoken and was astounded at the local populations' grasp of the French language. "Howard," he said in awe, "everyone speaks French here. Even the little kids."

Their first night on the continent they slept in an apple orchard 32 kilometers away, near the town of La Cambe. The locals in a nearby farmhouse invited them in, and it was here that Dad was introduced to Calvados, the local apple brandy, which remained a firm favorite of his. The next day the 2nd MAMAS traveled south to St-Lô, which Irish playwright and novelist Samuel Beckett called "the town the American Allies bombed out of existence." They occupied a nearby chateau and Dad spent several hours taking pictures of the destruction.

From St-Lô the 2nd MAMAS traveled to Alençon through countryside that was still a battle zone, a trip that took several days. Besides *Lady Chatter-*

*ley* they had a truck to transport their lab equipment, and when they couldn't find night lodging with field units they came across they slept in fields.

On the way Harry and Dad gave a lift to a US Army Lieutenant who was also going to Alençon. As evening approached he directed them to an Army encampment where they could sleep that night. When they arrived, the Lieutenant suggested Dad get out at the check-in point and make their arrangements while he and Harry parked the vehicle in a nearby field.

Dad protested, saying he could park with them and walk back, but the Lieutenant was insistent, so Dad got out and the Lieutenant moved into Dad's seat. Harry drove on and hit a landmine, killing the Lieutenant and injuring himself. Dad said it was a shame as the Lieutenant "was an awfully nice guy"[4]. They were issued a new *Lady Chatterley*.

When they reached Alençon they set up the 10th Medical Laboratory in a local school, the École Normale. The walls of the classrooms were covered with graffiti drawn by bored German soldiers who had occupied the area and which the 2nd MAMAS found funny. It was late August and Dad said the weather was beautiful and the food excellent. The region was known for their cheeses and Dad's group discovered Camembert cheese and the local cider. After the intense work of the past three months, he said it felt like a vacation.

Paris was liberated by the Allies on August 25th, and the 2nd MAMAS moved to Garches, a western suburb of Paris, where the 203rd General Hospital had just been established at a new hospital complex. The 203rd became the largest medical establishment in the European Theater of Operations with more than 3,500 beds and treated in excess of 65,000 patients for the duration of the war.

At the 203rd General Hospital the 2nd MAMAS set up the new ETO Blood Bank, which began supplying blood to the other hospitals on mainland Europe. All blood airlifted from the United States was now flown direct to Le Bourget airfield, in a Paris suburb, and delivered to the 203rd.

Getting medical supplies and blood forward to the front-line field hos-

---

[4] Dad was, like many veterans of World War II, stoic when he recounted his experiences. "You couldn't afford to overreact to things that happened. You had to keep going."

pitals was difficult. Reconstituted dried plasma was used at the 203rd General Hospital but, as predicted, distilled water proved much more difficult to source in the field hospitals which relied heavily on whole blood. The problem of getting it to the front lines was solved by the discovery of an idle squadron of 20 C-64 planes at Le Bourget. They were too large and too slow for active war work and their personnel were unhappy and frustrated. Arrangements were made for them to fly the blood and medical supplies forward to the lines and bring back wounded, usually five per plane. In three months they transported 30,000 pints of whole blood and 463 tons of medical supplies, while evacuating 1,168 patients.

From the airfields near the front lines, advance detachments of Major Hardin's specially-equipped trucks with trained drivers delivered whole blood under dangerous conditions in unknown terrain. Each refrigerator truck carried a refrigeration mechanic and a sterilizer mechanic as well as their parts and tools. They sometimes had to drive through artillery fire and ford streams when bridges had been blown up, only to find that their destination had been wrecked by enemy action or moved without notice. The drivers took pride in getting the blood through and showed consistent courage and devotion to duty.

In October blood needed to be delivered to the mobile hospitals supporting the 82nd and 101st Airborne Divisions in the Eindhoven-Nijmegen area of The Netherlands. The airstrip was located near Saint-Trond in Belgium and the road through the combat area was nicknamed "Hell's Highway". Blood trucks required tank escorts due to enemy sniper fire but luckily the trucks were never hit. After the war the drivers in this operation were awarded the Croix de Guerre (the Cross of War medal) by the French Government.

Winter began and the 2nd MAMAS settled in to work in Garches. Dad was quartered in an attic room under the mansard roof of an old house that had no indoor plumbing and no heat. He hated the cold but he knew he was better off than the Parisians, who were starving as well as freezing. At least the Allied troops were being well fed.

The American hospital began attracting many famous visitors. Entertainer Maurice Chevalier visited the wounded troops but got a cold reception due to his perceived collaboration with the Nazis during their occupation of Paris. The beautiful actress Marlene Dietrich was a popular guest, but by far everyone's favorite was the American ex-patriate, poet, and literary figure Gertrude Stein, who insisted everyone call her "Gertie".

Dad said Gertrude came almost every day to read to the troops. She had recently moved back to Paris from the small town of Culoz, near the Swiss border, where she and Alice B Toklas had lived earlier in the war and where she wrote *Wars That I Have Seen*. She and Dad spoke often of the fact that while the French countryside had abundant cheese, eggs, and flour, the transportation to get it to Paris had been destroyed. On one occasion she brought Dad a slice of a local Culoz cheese to sample and he shared some American chocolate she declared divine.

On infrequent days off Dad and Harry took *Lady Chatterley* on day trips around Paris. He remembered Versailles as being practically deserted, and particularly liked St Cloud. On a trip to Reims they met an American air crew who had found a captured German fighter plane they restored and flew themselves. Turning south, they stopped at Chartres before heading on to Cannes where ex-patriates from all over Europe were enjoying the winter.

Life on the French Riviera surprised Dad. He said it was like they didn't even know there was a war going on.

## "Everyone Speaks French Here. Even The Little Kids."

As the Allied Forces advanced towards Paris in August 1944—three months after the D-Day landings—the 2nd MAMAS followed to France to provide medical laboratory support for the wounded. Above: The apple orchard where the 2nd MAMAS slept their first night in France. (Image 12.2) Below: A nearby farmhouse invited them in to sample the local Calvados. (Image 12.3)

Above: Harry Lackey and Dad meet a local young man who, much to Harry's surprise, spoke perfect French. (Image 12.4) Below: Washing facilities were not always available, so Dad sometimes had to live the rough life. (Image 12.5)

## "Everyone Speaks French Here. Even The Little Kids."

St-Lô, France. Between June 6th and July 19th 1944, American bombardments ruined most of the city, which had been under German control since 1940. Above: The bombed-out remains of St-Lô. (Image 12.6) Below: The crucifix in the Saint-Lô Cathedral miraculously survived the bombing. (Image 12.7)

Above: By August 1944 the Allies had cleared a thoroughfare through the rubble of St-Lô. (Image 12.8) Below: Members of the 10th Medical Laboratory work in the Château St-Ló, where they also lived. (Image 12.9)

"Everyone Speaks French Here. Even The Little Kids."

Above: The Château St-Ló was spared the intense fighting in the town. (Image 12.10) Below: A bridge crossing La Vire river, which flowed through St-Lô, was destroyed in the bombing. The US Army built a make-shift bridge next to it. (Image 12.11)

Above: After leaving St-Lô the 2nd MAMAS traveled 110 miles (175 kilometers) south to Alençon. They traveled with their own rations and photography equipment, finding billeting with whatever field operations they came across. (Image 12.12) Below: Dad digging a foxhole on the way to Alençon in Normandy. (Image 12.13)

## "Everyone Speaks French Here. Even The Little Kids."

Above: Dad and Harry Lackey relaxing by the side of the road. Harry is wearing bandages and recovering from having driven over a land mine in a field. (Images 12.14) Below: A destroyed locomotive on the way to Alençon. Dad said that while the destruction of rolling stock was great, the rail lines themselves remained mostly intact. (Images 12.15)

Alençon is 110 miles (175 km) from Paris and it was here that the 10th Medical Laboratory and 2nd MAMAS were able to do their important work in relative safety. Above: The École Normale, or public school, of Alençon. (Image 12.16) Below: Laboratories set up by the 10th Medical Laboratory and 2nd MAMAS at the École Normale, Alençon. (Image 12.17)

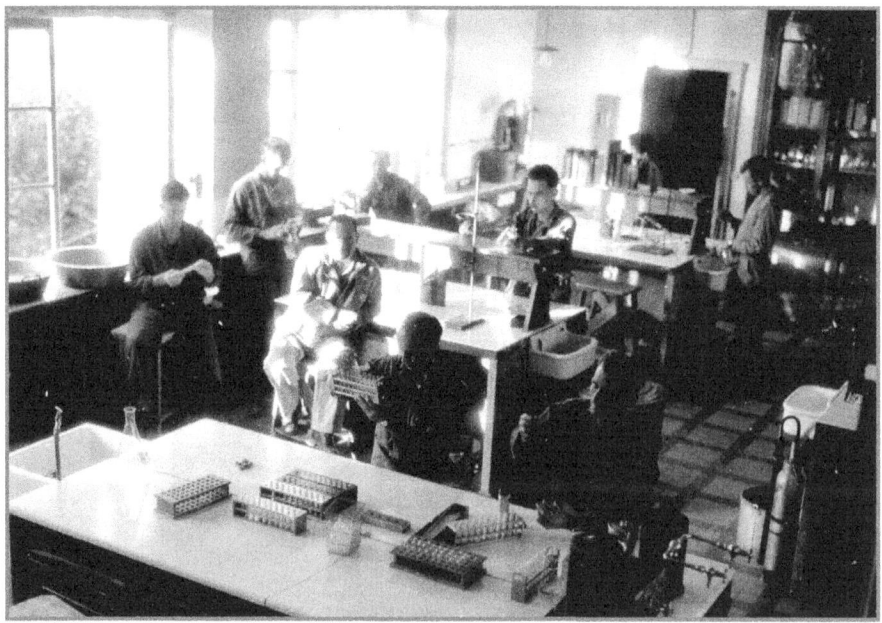

"Everyone Speaks French Here. Even The Little Kids."

Above: Graffiti, courtesy of the German occupation, on the walls of the École Normale in Alençon. (Image 12.18) Below: The Sarthe river which flows near the École Normale in Alençon. (Image 12.19)

Above: Dad and the 2nd MAMAS entered Paris shortly after the Allied liberation of the city, August 19th 1944 (Image 12.20). Below: *Lady Chatterley* at the Eiffel Tower. (Image 12.21)

## "Everyone Speaks French Here. Even The Little Kids."

Above: Winter in Paris 1944/45 was particularly unpleasant as shown by a deserted Pont Alexandre III. Dad said he had never been so cold and miserable in his life, but it was nothing compared to the suffering of the Parisians. (Image 12.22) Below: The US Army 203rd General Hospital at Garches, in the western suburbs of Paris. (Image 12.23)

Above: The building assigned to the 2nd MAMAS at the 203rd General Hospital. (Image 12.24) Below: Inside the cramped quarters of the 2nd MAMAS. (Image 12.25)

## "Everyone Speaks French Here. Even The Little Kids."

Above: The grounds of the 203 General Hospital in Garches, the largest medical facility in the US European Theater of Operations. (Image 12.26) Below: The Paris winter of 1944/45 wasn't all work and misery. The men visited famous Casino de Paris in the rue de Clichy. (Image 12.27)

Above: Maurice Chevalier—probably the most famous French entertainer of the century—performed one night, but received only polite applause. (Image 12.28) Below: The shows put on by the clubs and theaters in Paris were a far cry from the privations out on the streets during a cold and wet winter. (Image 12.29)

"Everyone Speaks French Here. Even The Little Kids."

Dad's passes that allowed him access to almost anywhere he wanted to go. (Image 13.1)

## Chapter 13

# Across the Rhine

By the end of the winter of 1944/45, the scrappy team of C-64s from Le Bourget had been replaced by a fleet of C-47s that ran a daily airlift of 17 tons of whole blood and medical supplies to the front lines. After the Allies crossed the Rhine in March, the armies were so far ahead of their established depots that the airlift was crucial.

Once on the ground the blood delivery detachments still faced difficulties. Hospitals were moved frequently and the information wasn't always passed along to the drivers, or passed along incorrectly. Stories grew of trucks driving around all night looking for hospitals.

As the armies moved east, the 2nd MAMAS followed the field hospitals to document their work.

"The front was moving so fast eastward it was difficult to plan our trips, so we gave up and wrote our own orders. If we heard there was something interesting going on, Harry and I would go see it." Dad said.

Dad and Harry traveled east through Luxembourg, then Duren across the German border, and through the Moselle Valley and Westphalia. From there they went to Cologne, then Mannheim, Frankfurt and Hanau. Wherever they went Dad noticed the richness of the German countryside and the destruction of the industrial complexes.

When asked if the locals he met had any resentment towards Americans, Dad replied, "In the cities, a bit. In the countryside they were just relieved the war was going to be over soon and they could get their crops in."

In Lippstadt Dad and Harry were assigned a large house with a beautiful grand piano that Harry would play every day. The owners were allowed to come back to clean the house and Dad spoke with them in German. They were cordial and said their son, who was an officer, was missing in action at the Russian front.

Nearby, the Allies had found an abandoned German field hospital and Dad photographed the equipment. Not much is known about the blood donor program in Germany, except that it probably began sometime in the early 1940s, and that only "true Germans of Aryan descent" were permitted to donate. The German blood transfusion laboratory in Berlin was subjected to heavy Allied bombing. Evidence the Allies found suggests that there was a shortage of blood and neither enough containers nor refrigeration capacity. Wounded German soldiers found in hospitals exhibited extreme pallor, suggesting that they had received little to no blood.

From Lippstadt Dad and Harry traveled to photograph army prisons and a concentration camp that had just been liberated. He never spoke of it, except to say that the American servicemen thought they were German army prisons.

One of the things that Dad remembered the most from the newly conquered areas of Germany was the endless waves of displaced people arriving and departing. They came from the east thinking things would be better in the west, and passed refugees from the west trying to go east. He said many of them were Russians and Poles.

As they left Lippstadt, Harry cut the wires on the piano. Many years later, when I asked him why, Dad replied "They were the enemy."

Spring 1945. The 2nd MAMAS began to spread out, following the Allied armies as they pushed east and south. Above: The beach at Cannes in the south of France on the Mediterranean coast. (Image 13.2) Below: Aerodrome at Reims in northeast France. This group of US Army mechanics recovered the German FW-190 fighter plane, repaired it and flew it. (Image 13.3)

Above: To get an idea of just how much munitions had been shipped from the United States to Great Britain and from there to the continent, this tank was the 50,000th shipped by the Chester Tank Deport ... (Image 13.4) Below: ...and the 4,000th troop-carrying car. (Image 13.5)

Above: Entering Germany, summer 1945. (Image 13.6) Below: Dad and Harry Lackey's house in Lippstadt, North Rhine-Westphalia. The owners were allowed to come back to clean it once a week. (Image 13.7)

Above: The house-owner's son, an artillery officer and commander of the local Hitler Youth group. He was reported missing-in-action at the Russian front. (Image 13.8) Below: Harry Lackey and *Lady Chatterley* in Lippstadt. (Image 13.9)

Dad went to photograph the Russian camp in Lippstadt. The conditions at the camp were primitive but safe. Above: The entrance to the camp in English and, below it, Russian. (Image 13.10) Below: A Russian couple with their baby at the camp. (Image 13.11)

Above: The US Army was determined to impose better hygiene standards at the Russian camp, which included men (and separately women) being deloused. (Image 13.12) Below: US Army kitchens at the Russian camp. Dad said there was unease amongst the local Germans that the Russians had more to eat than they did. (Image 13.13)

As Dad and Harry Lackey traveled east, Dad was particularly fascinated by the destroyed bridges over the Rhine. Above: The destroyed Rhine Bridge in Mannheim, connecting to Ludwigshafen (Image 13.14) Below: The temporary bridge built by the US Army, named the Ernie Pyle Memorial Bridge May 1945, after the legendary war reporter who had been killed in action in Japan in April 1945. (Image 13.15)

Above: View of the destruction and temporary bridge from the bank. (Image 13.16) Below: The Mannheim Bridge was destroyed by the German Army to slow down the Allied forces. Image 13.17)

Above: Cologne suffered terrible damage at the end of the war. On March 6th 1945 this bridge was blown up by the German army. (Image 13.18) Below: Amazingly the Hohenzollern Bridge in Cologne was open to pedestrians just three years later. (Image 13.19)

Above: Displaced people, moving east to west, hitching rides on US Army rail cars. Dad said there were just as many people going west to east. (Image 13.20) Below: The US Army came across a large German Army medical supply depot. They carefully inventoried and photographed everything. (Image 13.21)

Above: A captured German Army medical field rucksack. (Image 13.22) Below: A captured German Army chemical weapons field testing kit. (Image 13.23)

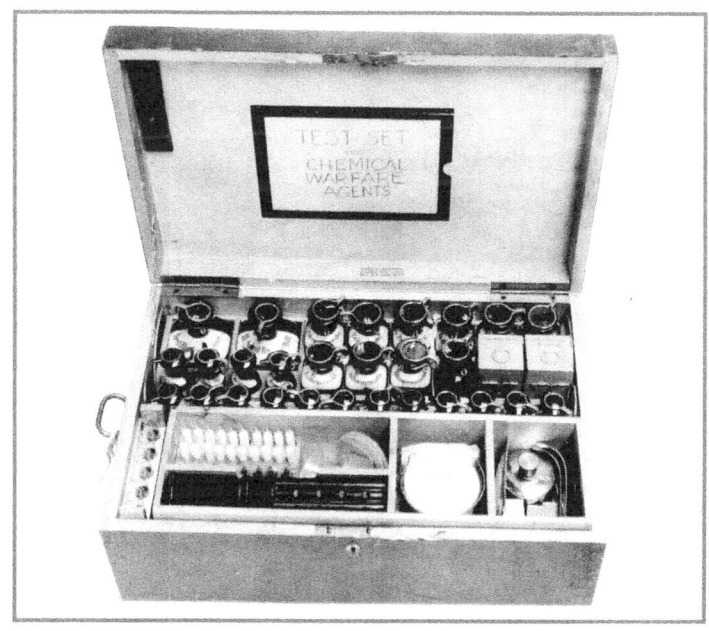

Above: What appears to be an apparatus to parachute medical supplies to troops on the ground in a shell casing. (Image 13.24) Below: The shell casing with parachute deployed. (Image 13.25)

# Across The Rhine

A German jet-powered fighter, the Messerschmitt Me 262, found hidden in southern Germany. The 262 was the world's first operational jet-powered fighter aircraft and one of Hitler's secret weapons. (Image 14.1)

CHAPTER 14

# He's carrying the suitcase

In the summer of 1945 Dad, Harry, and *Lady Chatterley* were in southern Germany photographing foot injuries in field hospitals, a topic of great interest to the Army Medical Museum back in Washington DC.

At that time, the post of Army Medical Department Commandant was rotated between the directors of the Army Dental School, Army Medical School, and the Army Veterinary School. The current Commandant was a dentist; his predecessor was a veterinarian. This dentist enjoyed a bit of sightseeing, but at that stage of the war jeeps and drivers were in short supply and he didn't have either. He heard about Dad, Harry, and *Lady Chatterley*, so he found them and suggested they take a day trip to Berchtesgaden to see Hitler's house.

"But the security is very tight there. Everyone wants to see it," Dad said. "They're not doing any medical field work and I don't have a pass."

"Don't worry," the dentist replied. "I'll take care of it."

Harry drove them south, stopping first in Salzburg to visit Mozart's birthplace, then began the climb to the Obersalzberg in the Bavarian Alps, which straddles the German-Austrian border. Soon they approached Berchtesgaden, where the Allies had established heavily-manned checkpoints. The dentist handed Dad a suitcase and instructed him to handcuff it to his wrist. Dad asked what was in it.

"Ten copies of the *War Department Field Guide for Dental Technicians*."

They continued on the winding road until they were stopped and the dentist produced his papers.

"Okay, you're good to go, but who's he?" asked the Military Policeman, pointing to Dad.

The dentist frowned. "He's carrying the suitcase."

At each checkpoint they were questioned, and at each it was established that Dad was carrying the suitcase and they were allowed to pass. Dad took color pictures of Hitler's teahouse on Mooslahnerkopf hill and the destroyed SS barracks.

They passed the burned out remains of Hitler's house, the Berghof, and drove on to the base of the Adler Haus or "Eagle's Nest" that the Nazis used as a meeting location. The building sat at the top of the Kehlstein peak, overlooking Berchtesgaden, and the dentist suggested they take the Kehlsteinhaus elevator up to the top.

Dad said the building was beautiful, although there were signs that American and British troops had already been souvenir hunting. They wandered around, ignored by the sentries posted in each room. It turns out they were used to important visitors —among them General Eisenhower, General George C Marshall, General Patton, Secretary of the Navy James Forrestal and General Mark Clark, and a young John F Kennedy — who had recently shown up to satisfy their curiosity.

They found themselves in Hitler's conference room and decided to take pictures of each other sitting in Hitler's chair, under the sign that said "Absolutely No Souvenir Pictures From This Chair."

The Nazi compound at Berchtesgaden in the southeastern corner of Germany, close to the Austrian border. Above: The entrance to Hitler's home, the Berghof. (Image 14.2) The remains of the Berghof, bombed by the British in late April 1945 and later set on fire by retreating Nazi Storm Troopers. (Image 14.3)

Above: The remains of Martin Bormann's home, bombed in the same raid. (Image 14.4)
Below: The remains of the Storm Trooper barracks at the Berghof. (Image 14.5)

The Obersalzberg. Above: Scenic Lake Königsee, now a part of the Berchtesgaden National Park. (Image 14.6) Below: The Kehlsteinhaus (also known as the Eagle's Nest), which was undamaged in the bombing raid. Hitler used this building for receptions and occasional meetings. (Image 14.7)

Above: The tunnel entrance to the Eagle's Nest, with sign reading "Field Grade Officers Only". It is said that when Eisenhower visited he ordered this sign thrown away. (Image 14.8) The conference room at the Eagle's Nest with American sentry. (Image 14.9)

Above: Howard J Francis Jr sitting in Hitler's chair in the Eagle's Nest. The sign on the wall behind him says "Absolutely no photographs sitting in this chair." Dwight D Eisenhower and other visiting generals autographed the conference table. (Image 14.10) Below: Victory in Europe Day, May 8th 1945, Paris. US troops in the Place de la Concorde. (Image 14.11)

Above: French girls swarm Harry Lackey and *Lady Chatterley*. (Image 14.12) Below: The celebration around the Place de l'Arc de Triomphe. (Image 14.13)

# He's Carrying The Suitcase

Above: The US Army filming VE Day celebrations. (Image 14.14) Below: During the winter of 1944/45 American ex-patriot and literary figure Gertrude Stein suggested Dad and his detachment might enjoy visiting the Paris Museum of Modern Art, which had just opened its first exhibit since the city's liberation. The 2nd MAMAS were astounded by the huge lines of people waiting to enter the re-opened museum. (Image 14.15)

Above: Inside the exhibition. (Image 14.16) Below: Two members of the 2nd MAMAS with a painting, perhaps by the Russian artist Leopold Survage. (Image 14.17)

Above: Visitors in the exhibition admire the works of art. (Image 14.18) Below: The Tuesday, May 8th 1945 extra edition of The Stars And Stripes, announcing victory in Europe. (Image 14.19)

Paris in springtime, 1945. Above: A crowd enjoying the sunshine at the Palais de Chaillot, Place Trocadero. (Image 14.20) Below: The Place de la Concorde, the largest square in Paris. (Image 14.21)

Above: View of the Trocadero from the Eiffel Tower (Image 14.22) Below: The city's most beautiful garden, the Jardin des Tuileries—with the Louvre in the background. (Image 14.23)

Howard J Francis Jr, Malvern, Pennsylvania, 1989. (Image Epilogue.1, collection of the author)

# Epilogue

Germany surrendered on May 8th, 1945, two days before Dad's 25th birthday. Dad and Harry spent the summer in southern Germany, and then were sent home in late August via Calas, just north of the Mediterranean port of Marseilles. Dad returned to the Walter Reed Hospital and was honorably discharged in December. His pay had risen to $132 a month, and he and the other GIs delighted in getting paid with a single $100 bill and 32 $1 bills. They would put the $100 bill on the top of the stack and flash the cash around Washington.

After the war, Dad was anxious to get on with his life. He applied to Penn State University and was accepted into the Chemistry PhD program, paid for by the GI Bill. He completed his Masters but left before he finished his doctorate after being recruited by Bell Labs in New Jersey.

Dad married my mom in 1961, and I was born in Philadelphia January 6th 1963. Dad was 43 years old and was guest lecturing at MIT in Boston that day. He always remembered it was the warmest January 6th on record in that city.

Dad was a professional chemist and we lived in Valley Forge, Pennsylvania, coincidentally on farmland once owned by the Francis family. In the 1970s, Dad became president of the International Microchemical Association and we spent every other summer in Europe for conferences. We loved traveling and he always brought his Leica camera along. He had many German friends, but he never returned to France.

After the war Dad and Harry's lives diverged but they kept in contact. They exchanged Christmas cards and met at least once in the 1980's at Harry's home in New Jersey. Dad often spoke of his 2nd MAMAS detachment friends with fondness, especially the unit commander Dick O'Connell. In speaking to World War II re-enactors who would request to meet him, Dad was polite but firm. "You're idiots. No one should want to re-enact what happened. But I guess everyone has their hobbies."

Dad retired in 1989 and passed away peacefully May 11th, 2007, the day after his 87th birthday.

The airlift of whole blood from the United States to the European theater ran from August 21st 1944 to May 10th 1945 and flew 201,105 pints of blood. The ETO Blood Bank in Salisbury collected an additional 130,635 units from April 1944 to June 1945.

Loss of preserved whole blood on the continent was very low. One plane crash on November 30th, 1944 destroyed 1,146 bottles of whole blood, but that was the only loss of its kind. By the end of the war, the efficiency of the blood supply was such that there was a ratio of 1:1 units of whole blood to casualties.

The Army Medical Museum today holds the collection of the work of photographers from every theater of World War II including Burma, China, India, New Guinea, Philippines, Australia, and Europe. By the first quarter of 1945, the first six MAMAS detachments reported taking 5,923 black and white photographs, 1,911 color, and 23,990 feet of motion picture film. The photographers documented a wide variety of subjects they encountered during the war. Dad said they focused on front line and evacuation hospitals and the triage techniques they developed, which were later used by the Army to develop the MASH units in the Korean Conflict.

By the end of World War II, medical science had accepted that whole blood should be used at once and without delay on casualties. After the war the accepted definition of shock became: "A situation produced initially by a decrease in the peripheral circulatory blood volume that is filled by a diminished venous return, an inadequate cardiac output, and depleted physiologic functions. The usual cause of these changes is gross hemorrhage." This definition stood for several decades. It was also proved that type O blood could be safely used as a universal donor. Science has shown that treatment with whole blood has become the standard of care for hypovolemic shock.

Perhaps the biggest heroes of the story of whole blood in World War II are the refrigerator mechanics. It is a tribute to their capabilities and devoted work that not a single major refrigeration breakdown occurred during the entire period of operation of the ETO Blood Bank.

# Epilogue

Above: The troop staging area in Calas, France, northwest of Marseilles, France. (Image Epilogue.2) Below: The troop carrier USS *Oneida Victory*, a ship that has a record of service only in the Pacific Theater of Operations. (Image Epilogue.3)

Above: Harry Lackey, Howard Cradick, and Howard J Francis Jr aboard the Oneida Victory. (Image Epilogue.4) Below: Troops boarding the *Oneida Victory*. (Image: Epilogue.5)

# Epilogue

# Acknowledgments

This book has been a labor of love by Dad's family and those who knew and admired him.

I am indebted to Richard Helmuth, who kept this project in front of me for several years and assured me Dad's pictures needed to be part of the historical narrative. Howard Newstadt provided a crucial beta-read that gave me needed direction and confidence. Georgina Waldman gave encouragement and valuable insight regarding medical terminology. Finally, without editors David Ballheimer and Angela Bell this book would be a mishmash of anecdotes that led nowhere.

Most of all, thank you to my husband Joe for his unwavering faith and support.

# About the Author

Marina Reznor lives with her family in Birmingham, Alabama. A fiction writer known for her Kingsbury Town Romance Series, this is her first work of non-fiction. Please visit with her at her website, marinareznor.com.

# Further Reading and Selected Bibliography

Alter, R. H, et al. *Map of the Pennsylvania, Reading, and Lehigh Valley Railroads, and their connections.* Philadelphia, 1884. Map. Retrieved from the Library of Congress, www.loc.gov/item/98688767/

Anderson MC, Colonel Robert S, Editor In Chief, Medical Department United States Army in World War II, *Preventative Medicine in World War II, Volume IX* Special Fields Office of the Surgeon General, Washington DC 1969. Library of Congress 55-63522

Bailey, John G *Army Blood Transfusion Service, Royal Army Medical Corps, Use of the Bat Symbol* 1939-1945 Typescript paper, Royal Army Medical Corps Archives, October 1973 https://wellcomelibrary.org/item/b19267058#

Coates, Jr MC, Colonel John Boyd, Editor In Chief, Medical Department United States Army in World War II, *Personnel in World War II* Office of the Surgeon General, Washington DC 1963. Library of Congress Catalog Card Number: 63-60001 https://history.amedd.army.mil/booksdocs/wwii/personnel/DEFAULT.htm

Coates, Jr MC, Colonel John Boyd, Editor In Chief, Medical Department United States Army in World War II, *Organization and Administration in World War II* Office of the Surgeon General, Washington DC 1963. Library of Congress Catalog Card Number: 63-60002 https://history.amedd.army.mil/booksdocs/wwii/orgadmin/DEFAULT.htm

Coates Jr MC, Colonel John Boyd, Medical Department United States Army, *Preventative Medicine in World War II, Volume II - Environmental Hygiene* Office of the Surgeon General, Washington DC 1955

Engle, Rob The Guilded Age in Reading Pennsylvania, Berks History Center,http://www.berkshistory.org/multimedia/articles/the-guilded-age-in-reading-pennsylvania/

Henry, Robert S *The Armed Forces Institute of Pathology, Its First Century 1862-1962* Office of the Surgeon General, Washington DC 1964. Library of Congress Catalog Card Number: 63-60060

Hildebeitel, Valerie *Eyewitness to History He Saw Figures In War's Final Days.* The Morning Call, April 8 1985

Jordan, Roger W collection, image of M/s *Elisabeth Bakke.* Chatham Publishing, London. https://www.awm.gov.au/collection/LIB50310

Kendrick MC, Brigadier General Douglas B, Medical Department United States Army in World War II, *Blood Program in World War II*, Office of the Surgeon General, Washington DC 1964 Library of Congress Catalog Card Number: 64-60006

King MD, Lester S *Blood Program in World War II.* Medical Department, United States Army, Journal of the American Medical Association, March 15, 1965, Vol 191, No 11. Page 158 https://jamanetwork.com/journals/jama/article-abstract/655141

Krantz, Tyler *General George S Patton Jr,* Undated. Puget Sound Navy Museum, Bremerton WA. https://www.pugetsoundnavymuseum.org/wp-content/uploads/2015/06/General-George-S-Patton-Krantz.pdf

Lawson, Siri Holm. *Norwegian Merchant Fleet 1939-1945, Ships in Atlantic Convoys.* Ms Holm indicates a source for convoy HX246 was transcribed from several documents received from Roger Griffiths - His source: Public Records Office, Kew. WarSailors.com https://www.warsailors.com/convoys/index.html

Montbertrand, Lois Shiner (2014) *203rd General Hospital, World War II* US Medical Research Center. http://hospitals.med-dept.com/203rd.General.Hospital/itinerary.php

National Museum of Health and Medicine, Otis Historical Archives, OHA 29. Curatorial Records: World War I and II Photography and Film 1916-21 and 1942-46 https://www.medicalmuseum.mil/assets/documents/collections/archives/2014/OHA-29-Curatorial-Records-WWI-and-II-Photography-and-Film-Records.pdf

National Museum of Health and Medicine, Otis Historical Archives, OHA 220. Museum and Medical Arts Service (MAMAS) Photographs https://www.medicalmuseum.mil/assets/documents/collections/archives/2014/OHA%20220.1%20MAMAS%20Collection.pdf

National Museum of Health and Medicine, Otis Historical Archives, OHA 220.1 Museum and Medical Arts Service (MAMAS) Photographshttps://www.medicalmuseum.mil/assets/documents/collections/archives/2014/OHA%20220.1%20MAMAS%20Collection.pdf

National World War II Museum *Fact Sheet: Blood Plasma*, 2017 https://www.nationalww2museum.org/sites/default/files/2017-07/blood-plasma-fact-sheet.pdf

Reynolds, Herbert Y et al. *Back to the beginning for the Eighth Evacuation Hospital in Morocco during World War II 70 years ago: Transactions of the American Clinical and Climatological Association* vol. 125 (2014): 154-69; discussion 170.

Robinson, Aaron *Storming Normandy in a World War II Jeep* Car and Driver Magazine, May 23 2019, https://www.caranddriver.com/features/a16580560/storming-normandy-in-a-world-war-ii-jeep-feature/

Sarkar, Brig Med J RS Armed Forces India. *Evolution of the role of army transfusion services in the management of trauma patients and battle casualties with massive hemorrhage* Medical Journal of the Armed Forces of India, October 2012. Volume 68, Issue 4, pages 366-370 https://www.ncbi.nlm.nih.gov/pmc/articles/PMC3862615/

Speer, Albert *Inside the Third Reich: Memoirs*, Weidenfeld & Nicolson, London, 1969.

Stein, Gertrude *Wars That I Have Seen* New York, Random House, 1945.

Taggart, Edward A, *Prohibition! The Failure of the Noble Experiment in Reading and Berks County (1920-1933)*, Historical Review of Berks County, Summer 1997 http://www.berkshistory.org/multimedia/articles/prohibition/

TIME Magazine *Medicine: Blood for Invasion* 24 April 1944 Volume XLIII No 17

Made in United States
North Haven, CT
06 June 2023